Keyboard Musicianship

Piano for Adults
Book One

Sixth Edition

By

James Lyke
University of Illinois, Urbana-Champaign

Tony Caramia
Eastman School of Music

Reid Alexander
University of Illinois, Urbana-Champaign

Ron Elliston
University of Maryland, College Park

Published by
STIPES PUBLISHING COMPANY
10–12 Chester Street
Champaign, Illinois 61820

Keyboard Musicianship

Piano for Adults
Book One

Sixth Edition

By

James Lyke
University of Illinois, Urbana-Champaign

Tony Caramia
Eastman School of Music

Reid Alexander
University of Illinois, Urbana-Champaign

Ron Elliston
University of Maryland, College Park

Published by
STIPES PUBLISHING COMPANY
10–12 Chester Street
Champaign, Illinois 61820

To Rita and Walter

ISBN 0-87563-444-3

Forward to the Sixth Edition

Keyboard Musicianship, Piano For Adults, Book One provides the first year adult pianist in colleges and private studios with unified musical materials which stress the fundamentals of musicianship. A well rounded musician at the keyboard reads well, transposes to other tonalities, harmonizes folk and popular melodies, plays by ear, improvises, can compose, and notate musical ideas. In addition, the keyboard musician plays pieces of different eras with taste and intelligence. The playing shows an understanding of how the body works at the keyboard (technic). This book is organized in a careful sequential manner to help promote all these various skills and understandings.

The Sixth Edition follows a basic plan for each chapter. As new musical elements are introduced, they are reinforced through a variety of musical activities. These might include analyzing (melody, harmony, form etc.), sight reading, harmonizing melodies, improvising short pieces, playing by ear and composing. Piano solos and ensemble works also reflect the new elements of each chapter (rhythms, harmony etc.) as do specific technical patterns for practice. Evaluation of progress is simplified with suggested quiz topics which appear at the close of each chapter. If students complete these quiz items with success, they are ready to move on to the next chapter. The quiz topics are especially helpful for the secondary piano student in the college who must meet certain levels of competency at the keyboard.

The text's eight chapters and appendices reflect a typical first year college secondary piano program curriculum. Normally, a first semester class (about 15 or 16 weeks) would cover Chapters 1 - 4. Second semester classes would then complete Chapters 5 - 8. Colleges on the quarter system would modify the coverage of these chapters accordingly. Teachers may find supplementary materials helpful. Those used at the University of Illinois at Urbana-Champaign during the first semester include *Early Level Piano Patterns, Vol. One* by Lyke and Heitler, and *Irving Berlin Melodies: Treble Clef Book* by Lyke and Kocour. Supplementary Books used in the second semester include *Early Level Piano Patterns, Vol. Two* by Lyke and Heitler, and *Irving Berlin Melodies: Bass Clef Book* by Lyke and Kocour. These books are available from Stipes Publishing Company.

The Sixth Edition of *Keyboard Musicianship, Book One* features a new section, *American Song Repertoire* which commences with Chapter 3. Songs by such American composers as George M. Cohan, Irving Berlin and Jerome Kern complement arrangements of ethnic folk songs. New composers who have contributed solos and ensemble selections include Céline Bussières–Lessard and Ben Blozan. Tony Caramia has added several new pieces for this edition.

Keyboard Musicianship, Book One is designed with the creative teacher in mind. Its organization makes planning, teaching and evaluating an easy process. Interesting lessons may be designed by teachers in either a piano lab or private studio setting. It goes without saying that the teacher is the key person in providing leadership, encouragement and effective instruction to help students become good keyboard musicians.

Table of Contents

Chapter 3

Chapter 4

Chapter 5

CHAPTER 1
The Keyboard, Rhythm, First Melodies and Pieces, The Basics of Reading, Notating, Listening, and Technic

Exploring the Piano Keyboard

On the piano keyboard, high sounds or low sounds may be produced. These sounds, or *pitches*, become higher as you play keys to the right.

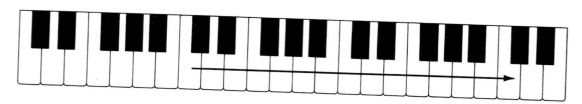

They become lower as you play keys to the left.

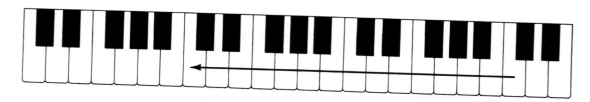

Find two black keys in the middle of the keyboard. Using your right hand (RH) pointer finger and middle finger, push down these two black keys, then move to the right and push down the next set; finally, move right to one last set.

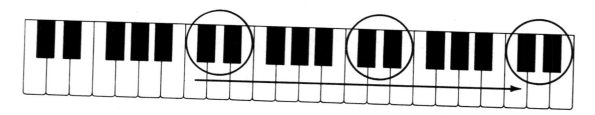

Using your left hand (LH) pointer finger and middle finger, find two black keys in the middle of the keyboard. Push these two black keys down; move left to the next set; and left again to one last set.

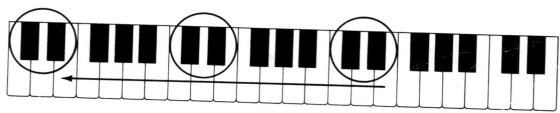

Finger Numbers

The fingers of each hand are indicated by numbers.

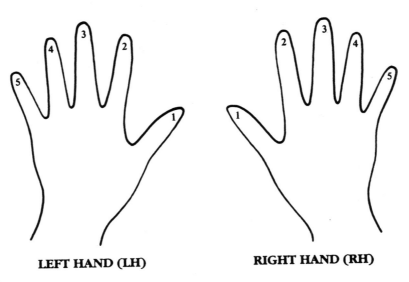

LEFT HAND (LH)   RIGHT HAND (RH)

Hand Position

Build a "bridge" with the knuckles of each hand. Allow the fingers to taper to the keys. Let the fingers not involved in playing rest on adjacent key tops.

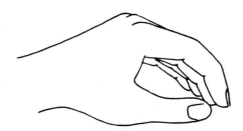

Finger Number Exercise

Place your right hand on a flat surface and shape the hand as pictured above. If possible, rest your forearm on the surface. Chant the finger numbers as you tap the following exercise. Fingers not tapping should be in contact with the surface.

1)	1111	2222	3333	4444	5555
2)	5555	4444	3333	2222	1111
3)	1133	2244	3355	2244	1133
4)	1313	2424	3535	2424	1313
5)	13534231			13534231	

Tap the same exercise with the left hand.

Tap the exercise hands together.

Black Keys

Find three black keys just to the right of the middle of the keyboard. Using RH fingers 2, 3, and 4, push down all three black keys; move to the right and push down the next set; and finally move to the right for one last set.

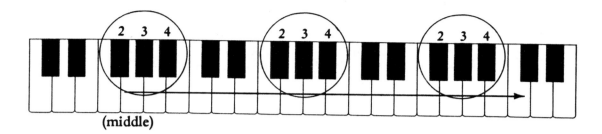

(middle)

Using LH fingers 4, 3, and 2, push down the set of three black keys to the left of the middle of the keyboard. Then move to the left and push down the next set. Finally, move to the left for one last set.

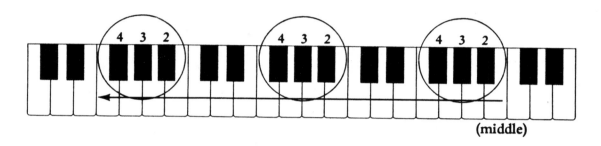

(middle)

White Keys

White keys are easily named by their relationship to the group of two black keys and the group of three black keys.

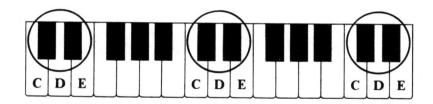

Staffs

Piano music is written on two five-line *staffs* which are joined together. The upper staff is called the *treble staff* and the lower staff is called the *bass staff*. For the most part in our beginning tunes and pieces, the right hand will play in the treble staff and the left hand will play in the bass staff.

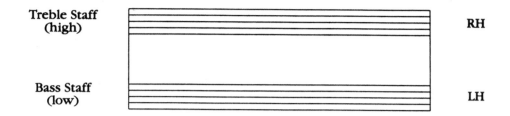

Grand Staff

When the treble and bass clef staffs are joined, the *Grand Staff* is formed. The *treble clef*, or *G clef* (𝄞) names its particular line treble G (above middle C). The *Bass Clef*, or *F clef* (𝄢) names its particular line, bass F (below middle C).

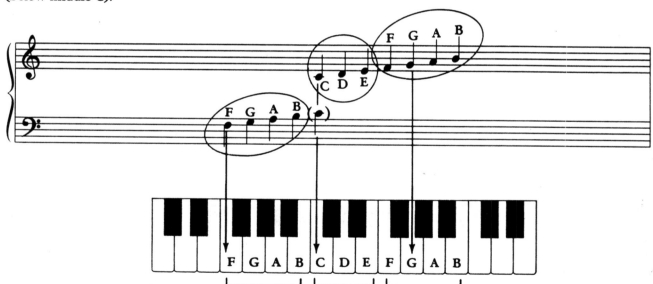

Line Notes and Space Notes

Music is written (notated) on lines and in spaces. Note that with line notes, the line goes through the middle of the notehead. With space notes, the note head is in a space. Notes can repeat, notes can step, and notes can skip. Note stems may extend up or down from the note head (♩ ♩).

line note   space note   repeated notes   stepping notes   skipping notes

Note Values

A quarter note (♩) lasts for one count. A half note (♩) lasts for two counts. A dotted half note (♩.) lasts for three counts. A whole note (o) lasts for four counts. Chant and tap the following rhythm pattern with both hands. Say 1 for ♩ notes; 1-2 for ♩ notes; 1-2-3 for ♩. notes and 1-2-3-4 for o notes.

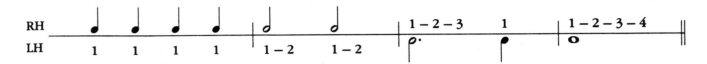

Measure Bars and Time Signatures

Music is much easier to read when divided into *measures*. Measures are marked off with single *bar lines*. The last measure of every piece has a double bar line. *Meter* in music is shown at the beginning of every piece with a *time signature*. The top number indicates the number of pulses in each measure while the bottom number shows which kind of note receives one pulse, or count. Tap the rhythm pattern once again with *each* hand; observe the time signature and measure bars.

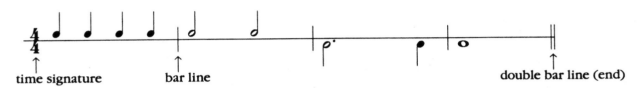

Playing Treble CDE Groups

Play the three CDE groups shown below. Start on Middle C. Count and say the names of the notes as you play. *8va* means to play one octave (eight notes) higher than written. *Loco* means a return to where the notes are actually written.

Leger Lines

Occasionally added lines (*leger lines*) appear above and below each staff. Leger lines facilitate reading. Play the melody below which utilizes leger lines above the 𝄢 staff. An *8va* sign below the staff means to play those notes one octave lower than written.

Reading From Landmark Notes

As you play the French folk song, *Au Claire de la Lune,* chant white key letter names in rhythm as shown in the first example. The repeat sign (:‖) means the tune is to be played a second time with no interruption in the rhythm.

Combining Hands

Before playing No. 4, notice that the RH is exactly the same as No. 3. The LH begins one step below bass F. Fingering in the LH is exactly the same as No. 1.

Three Marches

Chant the letter names in rhythm as you play. Practice the cross-over in the *F-C March* prior to playing. Memorize these marches for more rapid playing.

G-C March

S= student, T=teacher

C-G-F March

F-C March

Brisk, Rapid and Moderately refer to the speed at which each *March* should be performed. These are *tempo* indications. Tempo is the speed or pace of a composition.

Intervals

An interval represents the distance in pitch between two tones. Study the intervals below as they look on both the staff and on the keyboard.

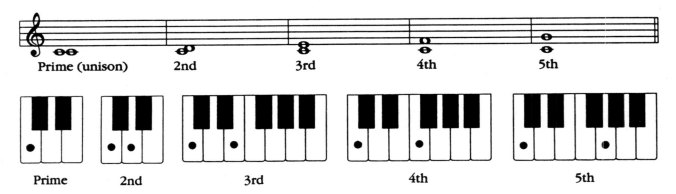

Prime (unison)   2nd   3rd   4th   5th

Prime   2nd   3rd   4th   5th

Intervallic Reading

The following melodies encompass either a CDE group or an FGAB group (with a few notes added). Some melodies are for RH, some for LH and some for the hands combined. A variety of time signatures and note values are used. Observe the fingering and count. Analyze the intervals which are bracketed. Chant note names in rhythm.

Dynamics: Loud and Soft

The sign for loud playing is *f* (*forte*). The sign for soft playing is *p* (*piano*). A slur (⌒) which connects noteheads is the sign for smooth playing, or legato playing. Lift the wrist at the end of each slur.

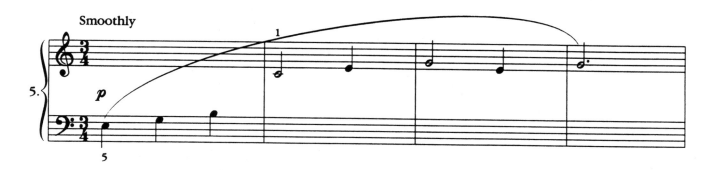

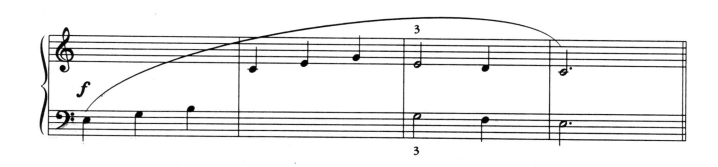

Accompanying

Play the accompaniment part (S) to *Roll, Jordan, Roll.* Your teacher (T) will play the melody. Study the handsets. Both hands will play in the bass clef. The time signature (C) means common time, or $\frac{4}{4}$.

ROLL, JORDAN, ROLL

American Spiritual

Note that RH fingers 3, 4 and 5 are not used. The *mf* sign means medium loud.

POLISH FOLK SONG

Ensemble

LAND OF THE SILVER BIRCH
Secondo - Teacher

Canadian
arr. Lyke

Slowly

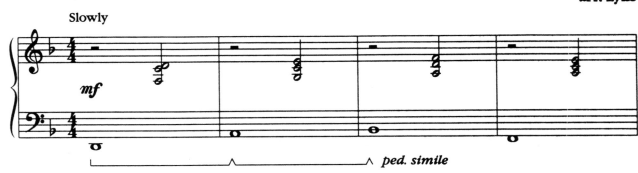

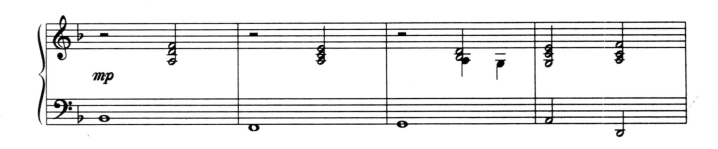

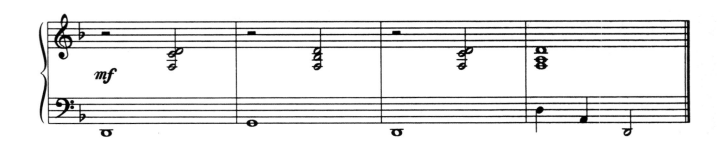

LAND OF THE SILVER BIRCH

Primo - Student

Canadian
arr. Lyke

Play both hands *8va* when joined by the secondo.

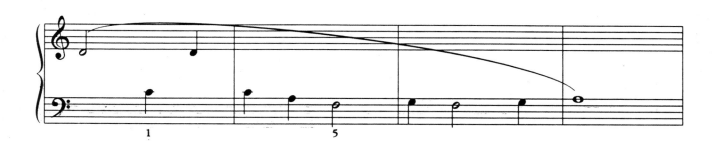

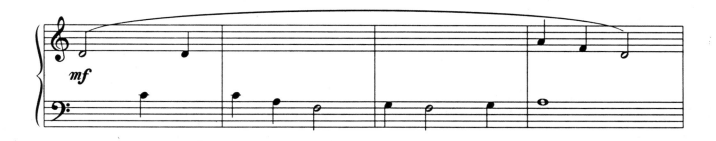

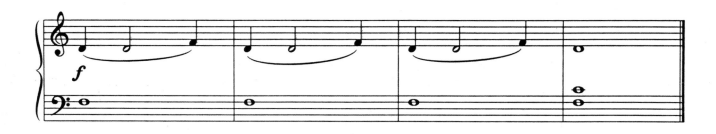

Repertoire

MIRRORING

Caramia

A CONVERSATION

Caramia

WALKING TUNE

Lyke

16

Rhythm Review

Tap the following rhythms on the piano fallboard or any flat surface. Chant note values as you tap. Try each pattern slow, then fast. Then play these rhythms on specific pitches indicated by your teacher.

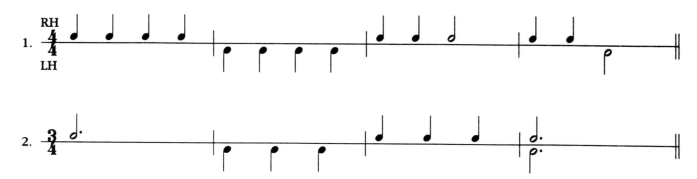

Interval Review

You will recall that an *interval* is the distance between two notes. In your pieces thus far, you have played all the intervals shown below. Study these intervals which are pictured as *blocked*, or *harmonic* intervals.

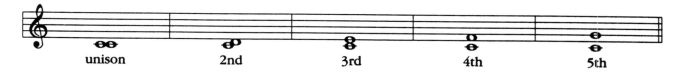

| unison | 2nd | 3rd | 4th | 5th |

Intervals may also be played as *melodic* intervals, e.g., one tone follows another. Study the melodic intervals below. Identify each interval.

Identify the intervals below.

Improvising

Improvise a short piece in 𝄳 time which uses ♩ 𝅗𝅥 𝅗𝅥· and o on the following tones. After playing various versions, notate your best effort and play it in the lesson. Start and end on either F.

HANDSETS FOR IMPROVISING

Ear Training

(1) Play back short melodic patterns sounded by your teacher. Starting notes will be bass F, middle C or treble G. Here is an example of what you might hear: (T) Starting note–treble G. (S) Listen–play back.

Note to teacher: make up at least six to twelve various patterns illustrating steps, skips and repeated tones.

(2) Identify and play back various melodic and harmonic intervals sounded by your teacher. Each will start on bass F, middle C or treble G. Here is an example of what you might hear: (T) Starting note–bass F. (S) Listen, identify and play back.

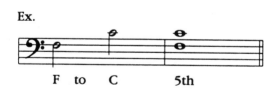

(3) Identify and clap back various rhythmic patterns tapped by your teacher. Here is an example of what you might hear: (T) ♩ ♩ 𝅗𝅥 (S) Tap back saying "1-1-1-2."

Composing

Compose a short piece in 𝄴 or 𝄳 using the handsets given above for improvising. Make your piece 16 bars in length (four phrases). Use elements of repetition and contrast. Your piece might work out as follows: phrase A, repeat of phrase A, phrase B (contrast with a different melody), return of phrase A. Notate your composition.

18

Technic

These exercises stress arm freedom and playing on the pads of the fingers using various finger combinations. Use these studies as *warm-ups* at the beginning of a practice session.

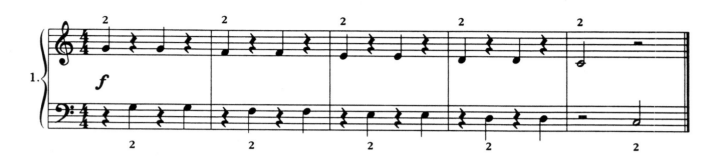

1.

Right Hand Alone

2a.

Left Hand Alone

2b.

Repeat with 12321
and 34543

SUGGESTED QUIZ TOPICS – CHAPTER ONE

1. Play one solo from pages 14 and 15.

2. Play the primo part of the duet on page 13.

3. Play an accompaniment from pages 10 and 11.

4. Block intervals in the RH from unisons through fifths. Begin on C (RH 1, LH 5).

5. Play all three Marches on page 7 at a brisk tempo.

6. Play an original piece on the patterns suggested at the top of page 17.

CHAPTER 2
Major Pentachords, Sharps, Flats, Naturals, Eighth Notes, Rests, Touches, Harmonizing With 5ths, Repertoire, Review, Technic

The Major Pentachord

Play the following two examples which illustrate an important structure called the major pentachord, or major five finger pattern. Chant the letter names in rhythm as you play each example.

C MAJOR PENTACHORD—RH

G MAJOR PENTACHORD—LH

The *major pentachord* consists of a certain step arrangement of piano keys. A *half step* is the distance from one key to the very next key. A *whole step* consists of two half steps, with one key skipped. H = half step; W = whole step. Study the diagrams.

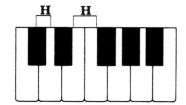
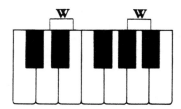

A major pentachord (major 5 finger pattern) consists of the following: whole step, whole step, half step, whole step. Memorize this order. Each pentachord starts with a keynote which names the pattern.

BRITISH TUNE

Before playing *British Tune*, identify the pentachord used. Tap the rhythms before playing. In addition, chant the letter names in rhythm.

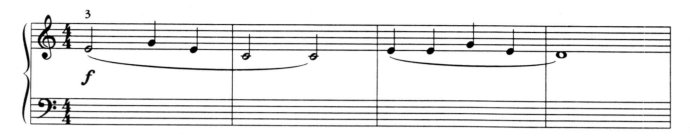

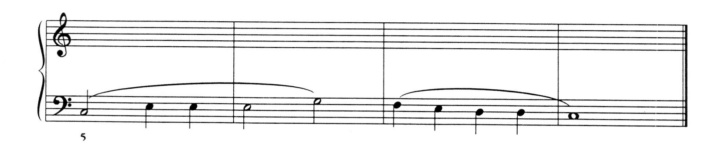

GERMAN TUNE

The quarter note which begins *German Tune* illustrates an upbeat, or anacrusis. Its value is subtracted from the final measure.

Sharps and Flats

A *sharp* (♯) placed before a note indicates *that* note be played one half step higher. It lasts through a whole measure unless cancelled by a natural (♮).

A *flat* (♭) placed before a note indicates *that* note be played one half step lower. It lasts through a whole measure unless cancelled by a ntural (♮).

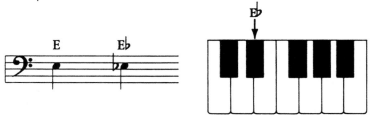

Study and play the various sharps and flats shown below. A knowledge of sharps and flats becomes necessary when building various major pentachords.

♯ Sharp: one key up from the closest white key. This may be a black key or a white key.

♭ Flat: one key down from the closest white key. This may be a black key or a white key.

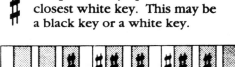

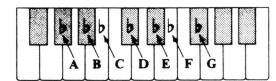

POLISH TUNE

Identify the pentachord used in *Polish Tune*. What sharp is used? Why?

3

LATIN TUNE

Identify the major pentachord used in *Latin Tune.* Name the keynote, spell the pentachord, check the arrangement of whole and half steps, tap the rhythm, chant letter names in rhythm, and play at a moderate tempo. Identify the intervals used in the melody. *mf* means medium loud.

CROATION TUNE

A *natural sign* (♮) shows a cancellation of a flat or sharp and a return to the natural (white) key.

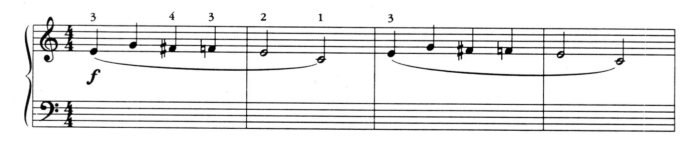

Eighth Notes

In meters with 4 as a bottom number, eighth notes (♫ or ♪♪) are grouped two to a beat (♫ = ♩).

Tap the following rhythm pattern from *Casey Jones*. Chant eighths "1—a".

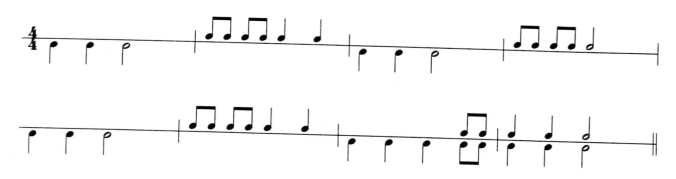

CASEY JONES

Quick tempo

*(Optional Accompaniment for *Casey Jones*)

For ensemble playing, the student part should be played one octave higher (8va).

BELL BOTTOM TROUSERS

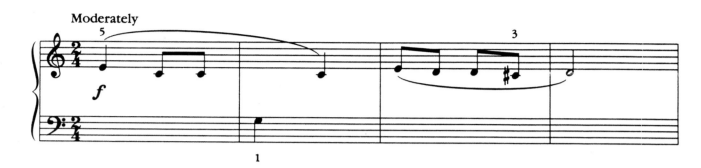

AUSTRIAN SONG

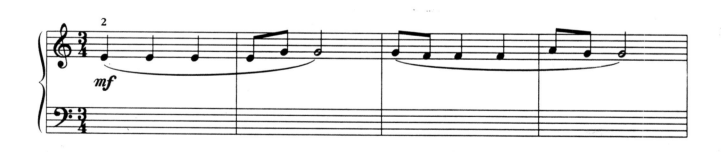

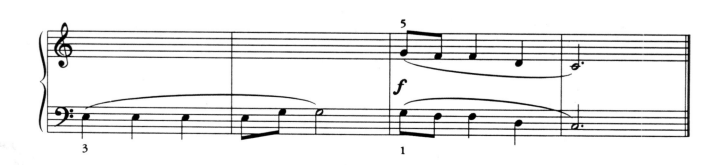

Rests

Rests are symbols for silence. Every note value has a corresponding rest. Study the chart below.

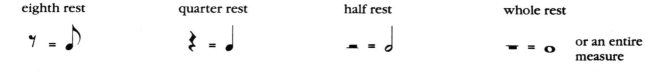

eighth rest   quarter rest   half rest   whole rest

Tap the following rhythm patterns observing all rests.

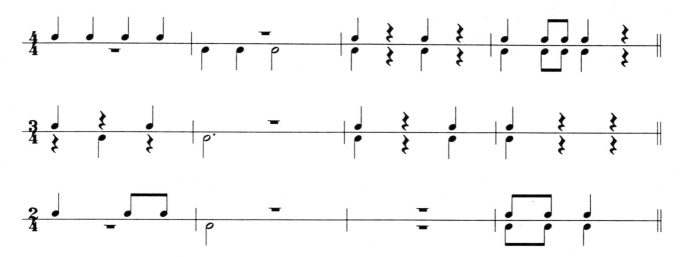

Blocked 5ths

Compositions often include the use of a LH blocked 5th as an accompaniment figure. The 5ths give a "hollow" sound. The curved line connecting successive notes of the same pitch (in the LH) is called a *tie*. The second fifth simply remains sounding for three counts. *Rit.* is an abbreviation for *ritardando*, an Italian term meaning to gradually play slower. The *decrescendo* symbol ▷▷ means to gradually soften. See Appendix A for terms and signs.

ECHOS FROM POLAND

Lyke

Harmonizing with Fifths

Harmonize melodies 1 and 2 with LH fifths. Notate the accompaniment of each melody. The 5th appearing in each first bar will be your guide. Add your own dynamics.

Danish

French

Staccato Touch

Dots above or below noteheads indicate *staccato touch*. Staccato is an Italian term meaning detached.

CAPE COD CHANTEY

New England

DUTCH MELODY

Appalachian

28

Music For Reading

Before reading the following studies, establish a routine which includes 1) tapping and chanting the rhythm of each hand, 2) chanting letter names in rhythm, 3) locating (by fingering) the starting positions of each hand from landmark notes (or C-D-E and F-G-A-B groups) and 4) playing slowly while counting. After reading, analyze the cause of any errors. Then play again.

For reading ease, whole rests (—) have been omitted from no. 2.

Practice Plan: When rhythm can be tapped and chanted securely, locate beginning pitches from treble G and bass F. Chant letter names *in rhythm* while tapping. Then play slowly chanting letter names. Finally, play at a quicker *tempo*, or rate of speed.

German

Practice Plan: Tap the rhythm of both hands and chant the values. Tap the rhythm once again and chant letter names. Locate beginning pitches by relating them to the C-D-E group. Play the tune slowly chanting letter names. Later, play at a quicker tempo.

American

Transpose to D

German

Transpose to G

WHEN I LOST YOU

words and music by
Irving Berlin

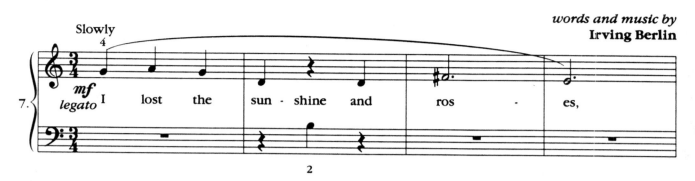

Slowly
mf *legato* I lost the sun - shine and ros - es,

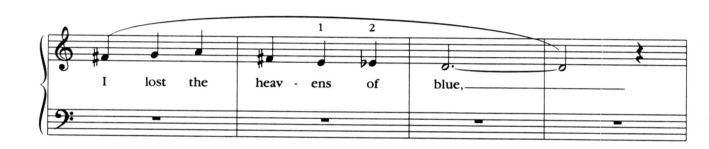

I lost the heav - ens of blue,____

I lost the beau - ti - ful rain - bow,
mp

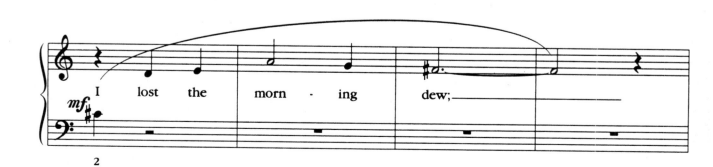

I lost the morn - ing dew;____
mf

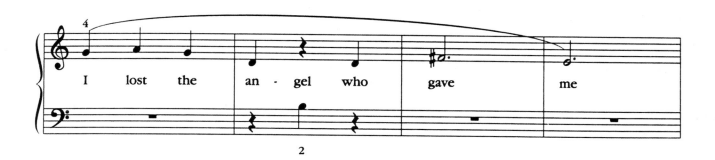

I lost the an - gel who gave me

sum - mer, the whole win - ter through,

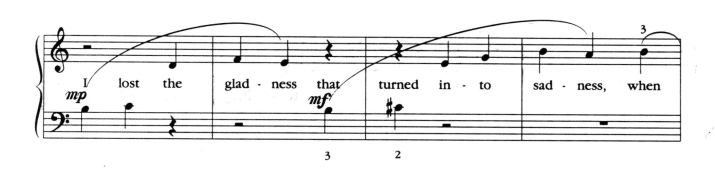

I lost the glad - ness that turned in - to sad - ness, when

I lost you.

PLAY A SIMPLE MELODY

words and music by
Irving Berlin

Won't you play a sim - ple mel - o - dy

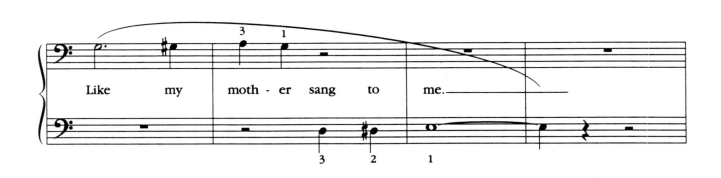

Like my moth - er sang to me.

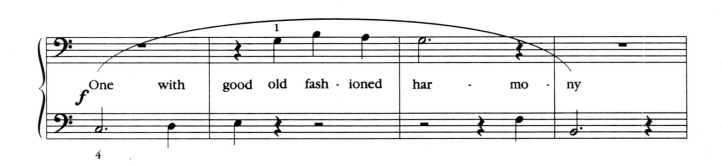

One with good old fash - ioned har - mo - ny

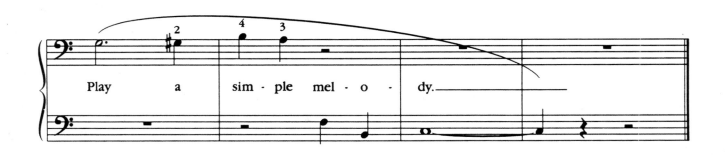

Play a sim - ple mel - o - dy.

Changing Hand Positions

It is often necessary to move a hand to a new position in order to have enough fingers for the notes which follow. Find such a spot in the following study. Analyze the LH intervals.

MY HAT

German

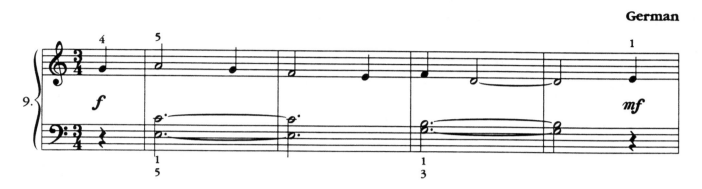

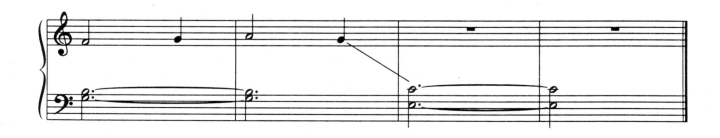

34

Ensemble

Tap the following pattern:

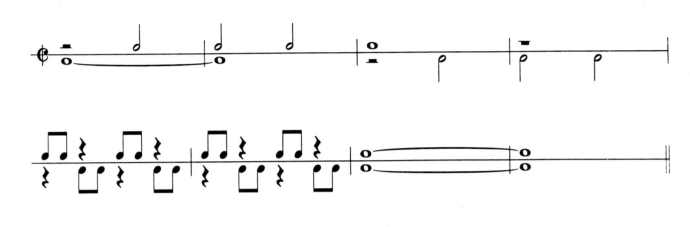

$\mathbb{C}$ means "cut time" or $\frac{2}{2}$ time. The half note ($\mathbf{d}$) gets one pulse.

WATERFALL
Secondo

Ben Blozan

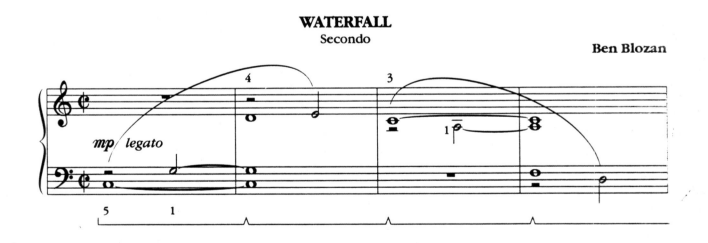

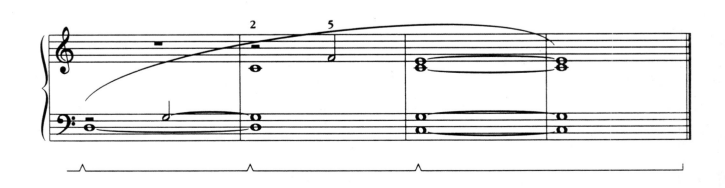

Pedaling

Waterfall uses the damper pedal, or right pedal. Study the pedal indications which follow:

depress pedal   keep pedal down   release pedal

Both *primo* and *secondo* may be played by students. The pedal should be handled by the secondo player. The

following marking _____⌄_____ means release the pedal and depress it once more. This technique

requires keen listening and coordination.

WATERFALL
Primo

Ben Blozan

THE BELLS OF ST. MARY'S

Secondo - Student

words by **Douglas Furber**
music by **A. Emmett Adams**

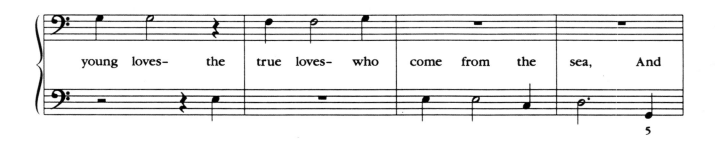

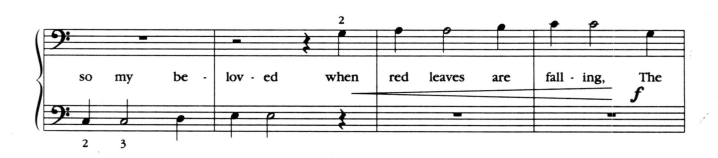

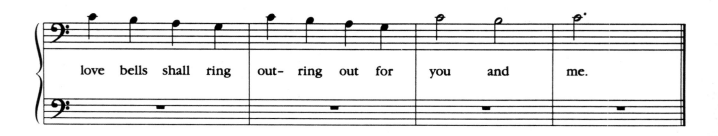

THE BELLS OF ST. MARY'S

Primo - Teacher

words by **Douglas Furber**
music by **Emmett Adams**

Repertoire

In learning the following pieces, develop an effective practice plan with the help of the teacher. Isolate difficulties such as shifts, problem fingerings, etc. for special study. Block figures, observe expressive markings, and play evenly. Even playing may require a *slow* tempo until all is under control. Above all, *listen* and make judgments about your own playing. Find sections, study what is alike, and what is different. Several pieces will require hands alone practice before combining hands. This will ensure secure fingering, proper position, and details of touch and sound.

SECONDS

Caramia

MOSTLY FOURTHS

Caramia

THIRDS AND FIFTHS

Lyke

MELODY

Köhler

LITTLE MARCH

Türk

Major Pentachord Review

Complete the exercises below which serve as a review of various topics introduced in Chapter Two.

Build the major pentachords indicated below by drawing letters on the correct keys. Number one serves as an example.

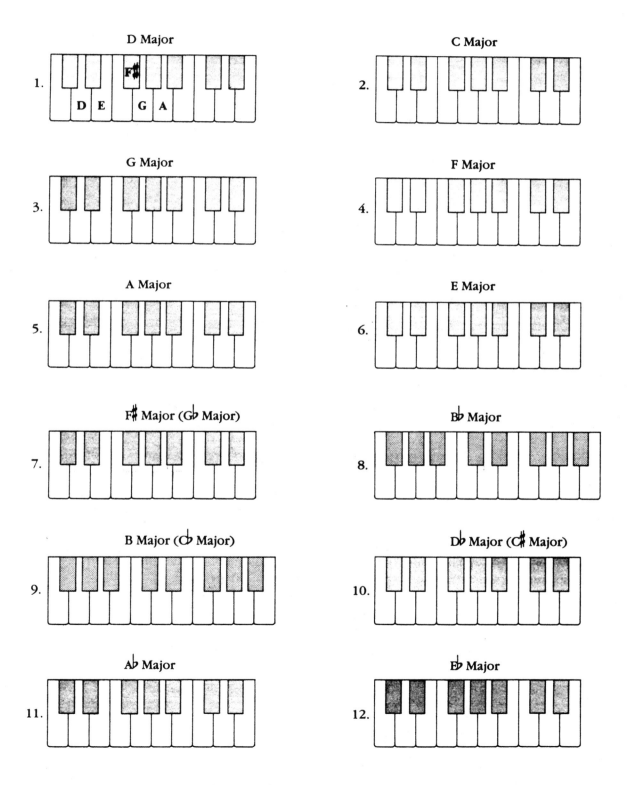

Improvising

Improvise two-measure completions to patterns 1-3 given below. These patterns have been taken from various tunes in the chapter and contain elements you have worked with: major pentachords, accidentals (♯, ♭, ♮) and intervals (unisons through fifths). Follow the instructions for each example. Improvising endings will help you understand the elements dealt with thus far. Don't worry about "mistakes" because there are none in improvisation. Simply listen and keep going. Use *repetition* and *sequence* (same idea on different tones) and think about moving toward the home tone (the first note of the pentachord pattern).

1. Improvise a two bar ending. Use the rhythmic values presented in the first two measures.

2. Improvise a two bar ending using any of the following rhythmic values: ♩ ♫♩ ♩. 𝅝

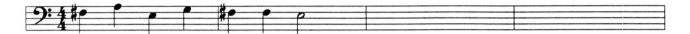

3. Improvise a two bar ending continuing to use eighth notes in the RH and a LH 5th accompaniment.

4. Make up an eight bar piece using a RH E major pentachord and LH 5th accompaniment. Choose a meter, tempo and mood and proceed. It will be best to confine rhythm in the RH to those values studied (♩ ♩ ♩. 𝅝 and ♪). Here is your handset.

Ear Training

(1) Review melodic and harmonic interval identification, unison through fifths. Your teacher will start on the first note of these pentachords: C, G, D, A, F and E. After the first note has been sounded, a melodic interval will be played, then the interval will be played harmonically. The student will listen, play back and identify the interval. Example: (T) Give starting note G, followed by B, then sound both together. (S) Play back and identify what is heard.

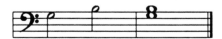

(2) The teacher will play two bar tunes which the student plays back. Here is an example: (T) Give starting note of the E major pentachord, then play the following example. (S) Listen, then play back.

(3) Teacher will have student clap back one and two bar patterns with eighth notes. Ex.: 𝄴 ♩ ♫ ♩ | ♩ ♩ ‖

Technic

The exercises and studies in this section demonstrate technical concepts presented in this chapter. Transpose each exercise as indicated.

Pentachord Preparatory Studies

Prepare for each position by shifting the arm and hand during each rest. Be sure to play each pattern on the pads of the fingers.

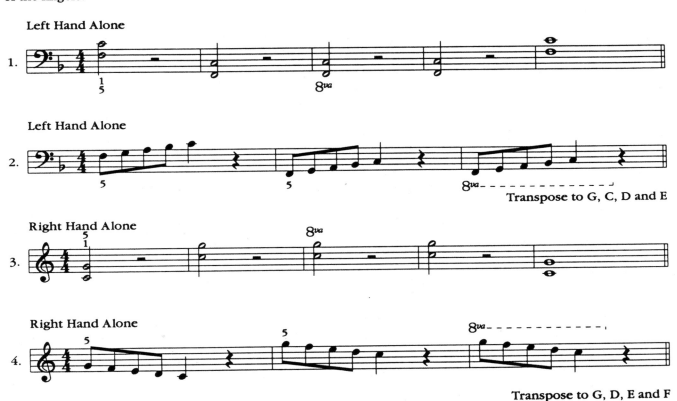

ETUDE FOR SECONDS AND UNISONS

Alexander

SUGGESTED QUIZ TOPICS — CHAPTER TWO

1. Build and play the major pentachords with the following keynotes: C, G, D, A, E and F. Use the example below in C. Then transpose to the other keynotes.

2. Play one harmonization study (using blocked 5ths) from page 26.

3. Demonstrate legato touch by playing *When I Lost You* by Irving Berlin, pages 30, 31.

4. Demonstrate staccato touch by playing *Cape Cod Chantey* on page 27.

5. Play one solo from the repertoire section, pages 38-40.

6. Play one duet from the ensemble section, pages 34-37.

7. Play an original composition which makes use of a RH pentachord melody accompanied by LH 5ths. See page 42 for suggestions.

8. Play any technical pattern which appears on p. 43.

CHAPTER 3 The Scale Structure, Key Signatures, New Pentachords, Tonic and Dominant Chords, Harmonization, Repertoire, Theory, Technic

SCALE SONG

Traditional

The Scale

Scale Song introduces a new time signature, ⅜, as well as an eight-note structure, the *major scale*. Observe the descending RH scale and ascending LH scale. Crossing over on finger 3 enables each hand to add an additional three notes to complete the scale.

46

The major scale will *always* contain half steps between degrees 3-4 and 7-8.

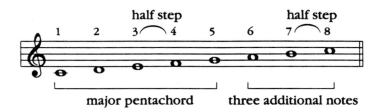

major pentachord   three additional notes

Key Signatures

If we try to build a scale on other tones, the same whole step and half step arrangement (as in C) must be maintained. Try playing the D scale by ear. You will find that an F♯ and C♯ become necessary to maintain half steps between scale steps 3-4 and 7-8. The discovery of the step arrangement of the major scale brings us to the reason for *key signatures.*

In written or printed music, the sharps or flats required to build the various scales are assembled at the beginning of the staff, rather than appearing before the notes. This combination of sharps or flats indicates the key in which the piece of music is written and is called the *key signature.* It tells which notes are to be sharped or flatted throughout the piece.

From the *key Signature* it is possible to determine the *keynote* or first note in the scale. In sharp keys, count up one half step from the last sharp to find the keynote. In flat keys the next to the last flat is the name of the keynote. Remember that the key of F has one flat.

Key of D   Key of B flat

Identify the following major keys from the signatures given:

D

Playing Melodies Containing The Scale Structure

Play the following melodies which make use of the scale structure. These melodies are divided between the hands. Identify the major key, place your hands in the patterns indicated and play the complete scale (ascending and descending) prior to playing the melody. A dot following a note increases the value of that note by one half.

Tap and chant the following rhythmic pattern.

WHITE CORAL BELLS

F Major Scale

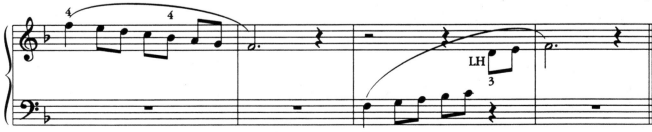

48

UNDER THE SPREADING CHESTNUT TREE

England

Scale Fingering

Many scales share the same fingering. For instance, the keys of C, G, D, A and E are all fingered alike. When the RH ascends, a group of three tones (123) is followed by a group of 4 tones (1234) and the keynote (or tonic) is played once again. When the LH ascends, the keynote is played and a group of 4 tones (4321) is followed by a group of 3 tones (321). Study the exercises below. Memorize the fingering patterns.

Practice *English Folk Song* hands alone first. Then play as written. Transpose this song to D, E, G, and A.

ENGLISH FOLK SONG

German Folk Song illustrates RH E major scale fingering in measures 1-4. In measures 5-8 the RH assumes the E major pentachord position. Practice the RH moves. Find elements of imitation in this arrangement.

GERMAN FOLK SONG

Building Intervals on Scale Degrees

Practice blocking intervals built from the keynote of the scale as shown below in the key of C. New intervals include the major sixth, major seventh and the octave. These intervals (major 6th, 7th and the octave) require a *stretch* of the hands. At first, practice hands separately, and then put the hands together. Transpose this exercise to all white keys. Then try it on all black keys, beginning on D♭.

INTERVAL STUDY
(M= major; P=perfect)

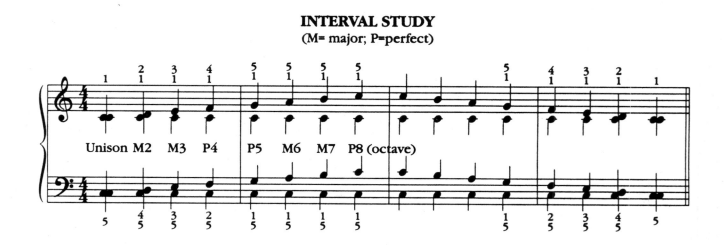

Exploring New Pentachords

In this chapter we will build and play tunes in the remaining six pentachords of A♭, E♭, D♭, G♭, (same sounds as F♯), B♭ and B. We have already played tunes in the pentachords of C, G, D, A, F and E. This occurred before key signatures were explained. Fill in the remaining letters of the A♭ pentachord. In this unison arrangement, check the LH position. The notes before the first full measure constitute an *upbeat*.

A♭ Major

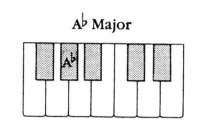

FRENCH FOLK SONG

D♭ Major

Fill in the remaining letters
of the D♭ Pentachord.

Folk Song

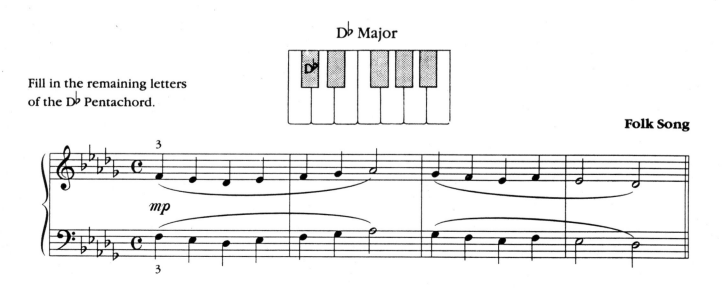

52

E♭ Major

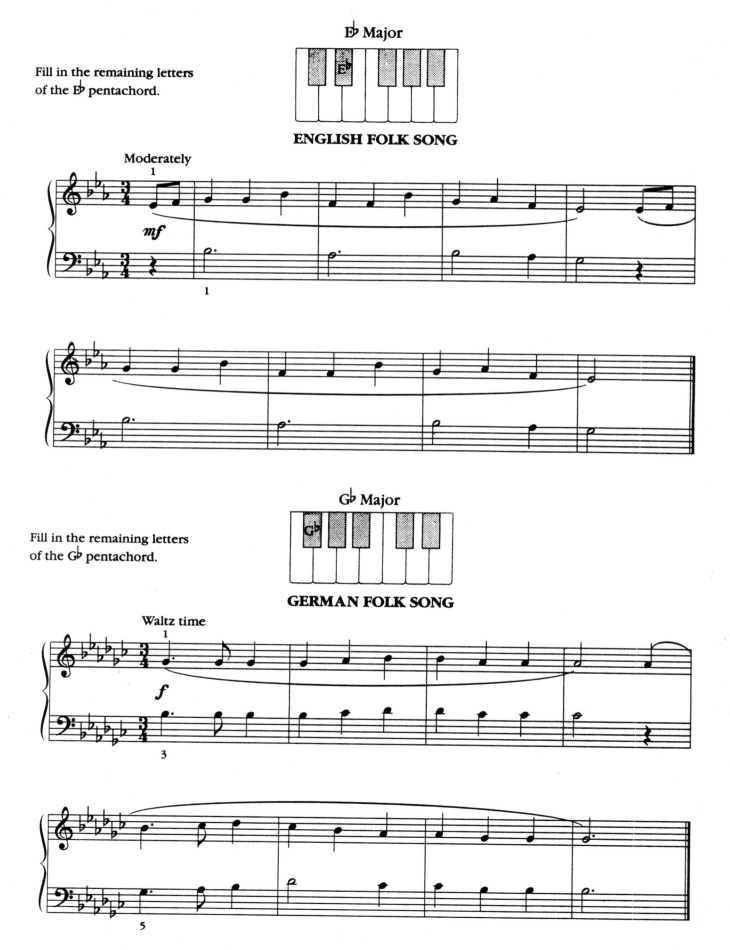

Fill in the remaining letters
of the E♭ pentachord.

ENGLISH FOLK SONG

Moderately

mf

G♭ Major

Fill in the remaining letters
of the G♭ pentachord.

GERMAN FOLK SONG

Waltz time

f

B♭ Major

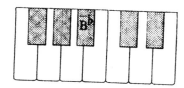

Fill in the remaining letters
of the B♭ pentachord.

FRENCH FOLK SONG

Moderately

B Major

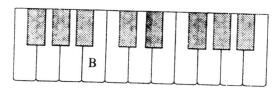

Fill in the remaining letters
of the B pentachord.

SPANISH FOLK SONG

Slowly

54

Major Triads

In a major pentachord (or the first five tones of a major scale) the first, third and fifth tones form a major triad.

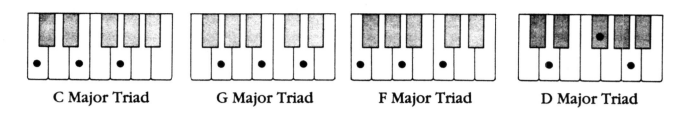

C Major Triad   G Major Triad   F Major Triad   D Major Triad

Many melodies contain triad (chord) outlines. Below are some examples. Circle the triad outlines found in these excerpts from folk songs.

The opening melody of *When I Grow Too Old To Dream* by Oscar Hammerstein II and Sigmund Romberg illustrates a combination of an ascending pentachord and triad outline. Use this melodic fragment as a transposition exercise. Gradually work through all keys via the *Circle of Fifths* shown below.

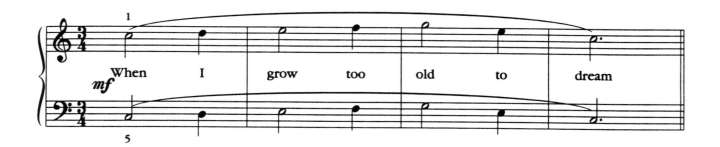

There are 15 signatures for music written in major keys. However, since there are only 12 keys on which to build, some of these signatures must be *enharmonic*. Enharmonic means same pitch, but different spellings. For example, F♯ is enharmonic with G♭. The relationship of the various keys may be shown by a *circle of fifths*.

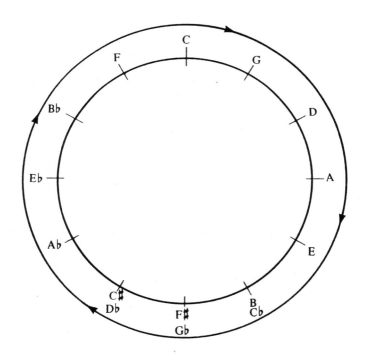

Key of C has no sharps or flats.

G—1 sharp	F—1 flat
D—2 sharps	B♭—2 flats
A—3 sharps	E♭—3 flats
E—4 sharps	A♭—4 flats
B—5 sharps	D♭—5 flats
F♯—6 sharps	G♭—6 flats
C♯—7 sharps	C♭—7 flats

Learn the order in which sharps appear in the key signatures: F, C, G, D, A, E, B. Flats are just reversed: B, E, A, D, G, C, F.

Accompaniments Using 5ths and 6ths

Slovak Folk Song I uses both a fifth and a sixth as accompaniment figures. Scale tones 1 and 5 form the 5th; scale tones 7 and 5 form the 6th.

Practice Plan: Tap and chant the letter names of the RH, then play. Practice the LH alone until moving from 5ths to 6ths becomes easy. Finally, combine the hands.

SLOVAK FOLK SONG I

Slovak Folk Song II uses 5th and 6ths for a RH accompaniment. Use the same practice plan outlined for *Slovak Folk Song I.*

SLOVAK FOLK SONG II

Harmonizing With 5ths and 6ths

Complete the accompaniments for the two folk songs which follow. Let your ear be your guide. When in doubt, study the melody tones. Non chord tones in the melody will harmonize with the 6th.

German

LATIN AMERICAN SONG

Harmonizing With Scale Tones 1, 5 and 7

Each scale degree has a name. The first scale degree is called tonic—the "home" tone; the fifth scale degree is called dominant and it helps define the key; the seventh scale degree is called leading tone and it obviously *leads* to the tonic tone. These three tones may be used to harmonize melodies. Take care not to double the leading tone in both voices when moving to the tonic.

tonic   dominant   leading
tone

T=Tonic; D=Dominant; LT=Leading Tone

American

Harmonize the following folk song using T, D or LT. Notate the bass line. Place LH finger 1 on bass F and LH finger 4 on C below bass F.

Phillipine

Harmonizing With The Tonic Triad

Using the full triad gives richness to a harmonization. Study the example below which uses the tonic triad in the RH as well as a 6th to harmonize non-tonic tones. Notice that the melody of the French song should be played louder than the RH accompaniment to achieve good balance of sounds between the hands.

Music For Reading

Before sight reading the following studies, establish the habit of 1) identifying the key signature, 2) chanting and tapping the rhythms in each hand (or both hands), 3) locating beginning pitches and fingerings and 4) playing slowly to avoid halting at any point in a study. Analyze errors after the first reading. *Trust your hands.* Transpose selected studies to the keys indicated.

PENTACHORDS

Russian

Transpose to F

German

Transpose to G

TWO VOICES

German Carol

Transpose to F

FRENCH CAROL

HARMONY

The Dominant Triad

A dominant triad is built on the fifth degree of the scale. The dominant triad, like the tonic, is often outlined in melodies. Study the examples.

The dominant chord has a strong tendency to move to the tonic. You have already used tones of the dominant chord to harmonize non-tonic tones. Study the dominant outlines in the melody below.

Study the harmonization below which uses the tonic and dominant chords. Capital letter names (G, D) indicate major chords. The capital letter refers to the root of each chord. (See Ex. 1).

Folk Song

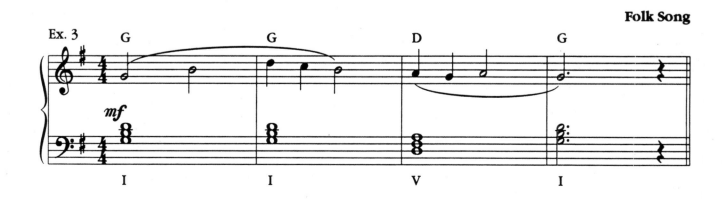

Harmonizing With Tonic and Dominant Chords

Harmonize the following melodies with tonic (I) and dominant (V) chords. The roots will be in the bass (lowest note). Later we will learn a smoother way to connect these chords. Notate the accompaniment in the blank LH measures.

Ensemble

ORANGES AND LEMONS
Secondo—Teacher

arr. Lyke

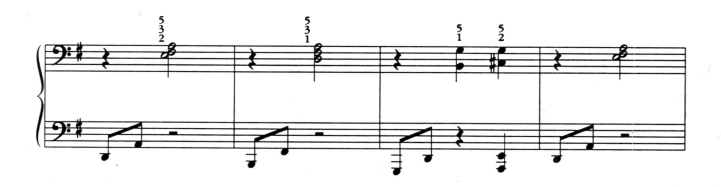

D.C. al fine

D.C. *al fine* means go back to the beginning and play to the place marked *fine*.

ORANGES AND LEMONS
Primo—Student

arr. Lyke

D.C. *al fine*

CAMPTOWN RACES
Secondo—Teacher

Stephen Foster
arr. Heitler and Lyke

Clip along

CAMPTOWN RACES
Primo—Student

Stephen Foster
arr. Heitler and Lyke

These signs tell you to repeat a section. At the end of the repetition,
skip the first ending and play the second ending.

COME TO THE FAIR
Secondo—Teacher

words by **Helen Taylor**
music by **Easthope Martin**
arr. Lyke

Moderately bright

COME TO THE FAIR
Primo—Student

words by **Helen Taylor**
music by **Easthope Martin**
arr. Lyke

Moderately bright

The sun is a - shin - ing to wel - come the day,

Heigh - ho! come to the fair! The

folk are al sing - ing so mer - ry and gay,

Heigh - ho! come to the fair! All the

stalls on the green are as fine as can be with

American Song Repertoire

Cohan's WWI song *Over There* contains some rhythms which are syncopated. This occurs when the normal accent is shifted.

Note the use of the G chord outline and the imitative LH. Study the LH part carefully. Identify the intervals.

OVER THERE

words and music by
George M. Cohan
arr. Lyke

74

Sometimes eighth notes "swing". In popular music and jazz the beat is divided into a *three* feeling, ♩ = ♩♩♩.
When playing eighths, as in the Kern song below, ♪♪♪♩ ♩ ♩ becomes ♩ ♪♩ ♪♩ ♩ | 𝅝 ‖ .

HOW'D YOU LIKE TO SPOON WITH ME?

words by **Edward Laska**
music by **Jerome Kern**
arr. Lyke

How'd you like to spoon with me? How'd you like to spoon with me?

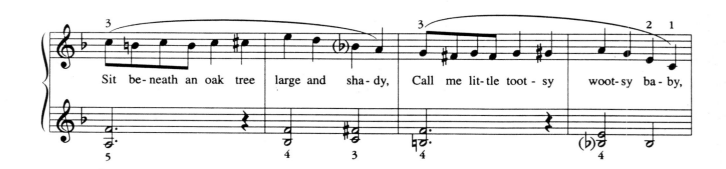

Sit be-neath an oak tree large and sha-dy, Call me lit-tle toot-sy woot-sy ba-by,

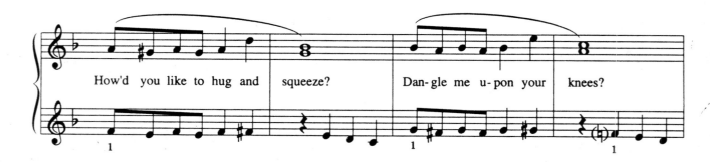

How'd you like to hug and squeeze? Dan-gle me u-pon your knees?

How'd you like to be my lov-ey dov-ey? How'd you like to spoon with me? me?

Repertoire

Compositions in this section contain the main focus of this chapter: scales, triads, various touches, intervals within an eight note range and playing in various keys. Italian terms are now used to define tempos. Consult the glossary. Analyze scale and chord patterns.

ALLEGRO

Türk

ALLEGRETTO

Türk

RUSSIAN DANCE

Goedicke

THEME

Kabalevsky

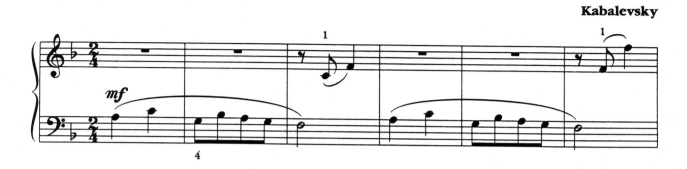

FANFARE

Czerny

SCALE STUDY

Gurlitt

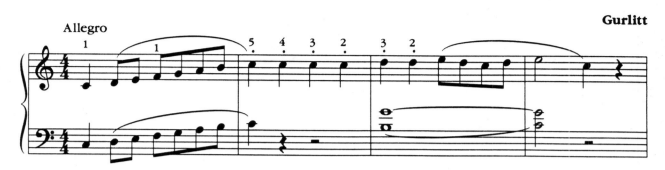

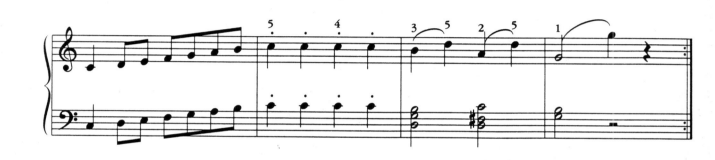

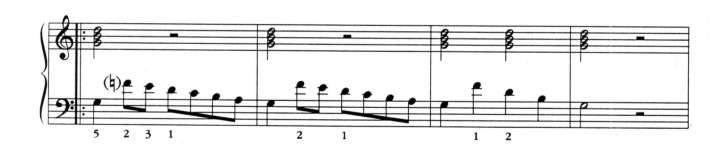

PATTERNS

Caramia

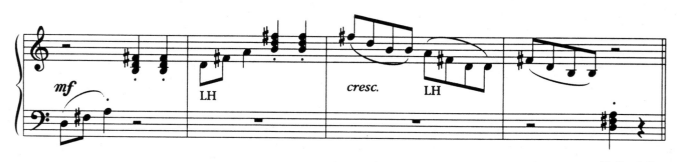

D.C. al fine

DANCE

Gurlitt

Scale and Key Signature Review

Notate the following major scales which use sharps. After writing the scale with the correct whole and half step patterns, place the sharps on the staff and give the proper key signature. See the G major scale as an example.

G major

82

Notate the following major scales which use flats. Then write the correct key signature. See the F major scale as an example.

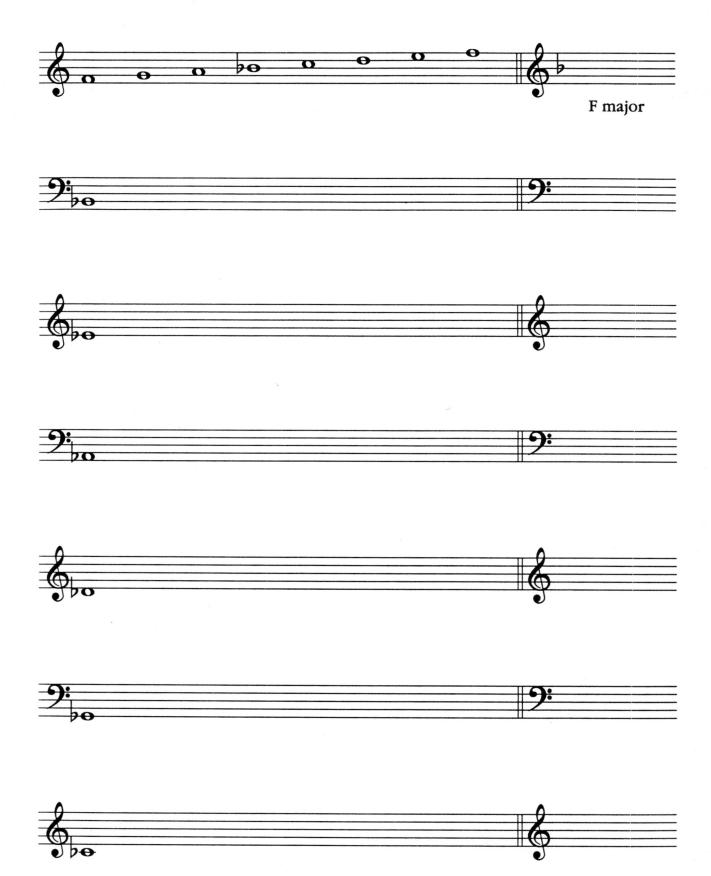

F major

Improvising

Improvise completions to the question phrases given below. These patterns have been taken from various tunes used in this chapter and emphasize the following elements: scale line melodies, 6ths, 7ths and octaves plus playing in various keys (tonalities). The question phrases will be four bars in length; make your answers correspond to this length.

Ear Training

1) As your teacher sounds various intervals, identify them (unisons through the octaves with a special focus on 6ths, 7ths, and octaves). 2) Distinguish the sound of a triad as opposed to the sound of a 3rd or 5th. 3) Play back two bar phrases which your teacher will sound twice. An example follows.

Technic

Play the following pentachord/triad study on all white key patterns (C, D, E, F, G, A and B).

1.

continue in D

2.   Play the white key scales of C, G, D, A and E. These are fingered alike. Consult page 49 for these fingerings.

SUGGESTED QUIZ TOPICS — CHAPTER THREE

1.   Be able to identify any major key from its signature.

2.   Be able to construct a major scale starting on any tone.

3.   Block intervals through the octave. Begin on the keynote of the scale (see page 50).

4.   Be able to build a major pentachord beginning on any note. Spell it correctly.

5.   Build a major triad on any beginning note.

6.   Demonstrate harmonization skill by playing the example at the bottom of page 58.

7.   Be able to play the tonic and dominant triad in any key.

8.   Play one ensemble part from pages 64-71.

9.   Play one American Song from pages 72-74.

10.   Play one solo from pages 75-80.

4 The Minor Pentachord, Minor Triads, 6/8 Meter, Sixteenth Notes, Chord Symbols, Harmonization, Chording Accompaniments, Repertoire, Technic

Compare the C major scale with the most common form of the minor scale, the *harmonic minor*. Scale steps 3 and 6 are lowered one half step in this minor scale. All minor scales share a key signature with a major scale. The lowered third step of the minor scale is "borrowed" from the major scale which best fits its structure. Other forms of the minor scale are explored in a later chapter.

C minor Spiritual Melody (GO DOWN MOSES)

The Minor Pentachord

We have learned the construction of the pentachord in major as: whole step, whole step, half step, whole step. This particular order of steps forms the first five notes of the major scale. *Major* is a quality and its sound is associated with *brightness*. The *minor* quality, by contrast, is associated with *mournfulness* or *sadness*. It differs from the major pattern in only one way: its third note is one-half step lower.

The Minor Triad

Play the major pentachord ascending and descending. Repeat it, but lower the 3rd tone by a half step. Then play the minor triad as shown.

Transpose to all white keys,
then to all black keys.

86

Minor Melodies With Accompaniments

The following minor melodies stress accompaniment figures using 5ths and 6ths and the tonic minor triad. Before playing, practice the LH part. Remember that the minor key signature is determined by the middle note of the minor triad or by counting up one and a half steps from the keynote.

Example

LETTISH FOLK SONG

HUNGARIAN FOLK SONG

Transpose to F minor

Lento

German

3.

In the *French Folk Song* below, isolate the RH part, the last half of bar 2 through the downbeat of bar 4. *Practice the finger cross and thumb under movements.* In addition, isolate the RH part, the last half of bar 6 through bar 8. *Practice the finger stretch.*

FRENCH FOLK SONG

Adagio

4.

POLISH FOLK SONG

In *British Folk Song* take special care with the fingering which involves stretches and shifts to new patterns.

BRITISH FOLK SONG

Minor Pentachord Reading

Analyze and sight read the following melodies which lie within the minor pentachord in each hand. Be sure to establish the minor key by identifying the final note of the melody. Double check by counting down one and one-half steps from the keynote of the *shared* major key. For example, number one has a G major key signature, but an analysis of the melody clearly establishes E minor (one and one-half steps down from G). Follow the usual reading routine by playing the pattern in ascending and descending form, singing or saying letter names and chanting the rhythm if it poses a problem. Look for patterns which repeat. Observe touch and dynamic markings. Transpose the melodies to the suggested keys.

Russian

Transpose to D minor

Bulgarian

Transpose to G minor

British

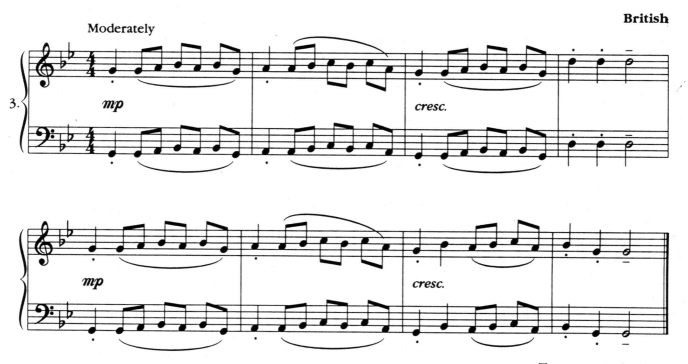

Transpose to A minor

90

Adagio

Latvian

Transpose to G minor

French

Transpose to C minor

Allegro

French

Transpose to A minor

Harmonization in Minor Keys with the Tonic, Dominant and Leading Tones

Harmonize the following melodies using the tonic, dominant or leading tone in the bass. Analyze the key of each tune. Complete each bass line.

Lettish

Carol

Czech

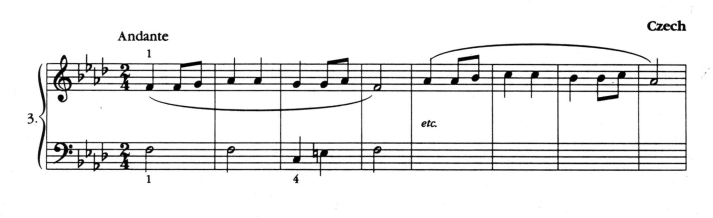

Major and Minor Triads Used in Lead Sheet Harmonization

You have already built major and minor triads in various exercises involving pentachords. Review these patterns in a few keys.

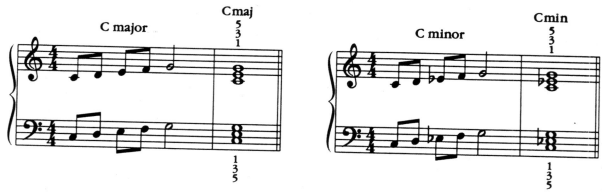

Major and minor triads may be symbolized by letter names followed by a designation of quality, such as major or minor. A capital letter, C for example, indicates C major. Sometimes this is symbolized as Cmaj. A minor triad is symbolized by a capital letter and the abbreviation m, or min for minor: Cmin. You now will be able to supply LH accompaniments to tunes by looking at the tune only and reacting to chord symbols notated above the melody line. One needs to change the chord only when a new symbol appears. Otherwise, one should retain the same chord. Study the example shown below which illustrates a *lead line*: melody plus chord symbols. Fill in the blank LH measures.

Lead Lines

Realize the following lead lines with approproate LH harmony. All chords will be in root position. Later, we will learn smoother transitions from chord to chord by using inversions. Study the example below which shows root position and inversions of a triad. The letter following the slash indicates the lowest note.

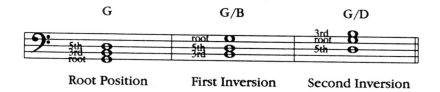

An accent (>) above or below a note means to give that note an extra stress.

MEADOWLANDS

Russian

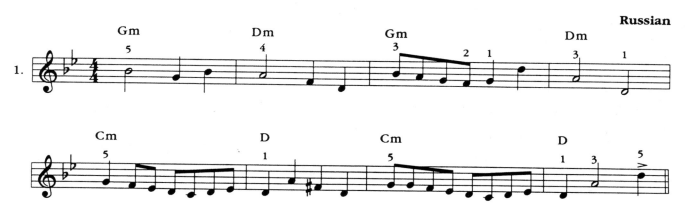

LITTLE BROWN JUG

FRENCH CAROL

6/8 Meter

In 6/8 meter, the top number shows how many eighth notes are in a measure. In 6/8 meter it is important to feel pulse of "two to the bar." In other words, ♩. becomes the pulse. 6/8 is a *compound meter* because the subdivision of the pulse is three eighth notes. Other compound meters include 9/8 and 12/8. Tap and count the following rhythmic patterns.

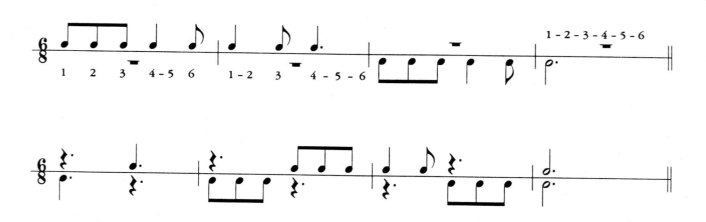

Acciaccatura

A very short grace note ♪ which takes place in the harmony it precedes. Play all three LH notes in measures 1-6; lift the second finger quickly to produce a bagpipe effect.

PAT WORKS ON THE RAILWAY

Two French Folk Songs in ⁶⁄₈ Meter

Practice each arrangement hands alone to grasp the correct notes, fingering and most especially, rhythm. The second tune requires the right hand to shift to a different pattern midway through the arrangement.

FRENCH FOLK SONG I

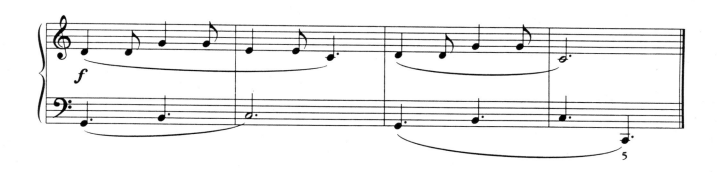

FRENCH FOLK SONG II

Sight Reading

Analyze the keys in the following arrangements. As always, tap the rhythms in each hand before reading.

Swedish

Transpose to G minor

French

German

Spiritual

English

Sixteenth Notes

Four sixteenth notes are grouped to the beat in meters with 4 as a bottom number. Two sixteenth notes fill the time of one eighth note. Dotted eighth notes followed by a sixteenth note may be felt as an eighth note tied to the first of two sixteenth notes which follow. Study the two examples below.

Rhythm Patterns

Tap the following rhythm patterns which involve sixteenth notes.

KOOKBURRA

Australian

D.C. al fine means go back to the beginning and play to the spot marked *fine*.

SKYE BOAT SONG

Scottish

D.C. al fine

*Chord symbols are provided for the teacher to provide an accompaniment.

Zum Gali Gali's harmony conists of two chords:
Notice the inversion of A minor and how smoothly
Em moves to Am in its second inversion (5th in
the bass).

ZUM GALI GALI

Israeli

OLD BRASS WAGON

American

POLISH MELODY

ALOUETTE

French Canadian

D.C. al fine

102

Chording an Accompaniment

Chords may be spread out between the two hands, with the LH supplying a bass note and the RH filling out the harmony. This creates a better *piano style* as opposed to the LH triads and RH melody. Study the chords below which will be used to create the remainder of the accompaniment for *Clementine*. Notate the accompaniment.

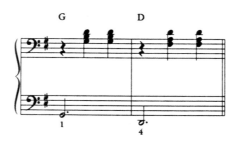

CLEMENTINE

Teacher part *8va* throughout.

United States

In a cav - ern, in a can - yon, Ex - ca - vat - ing for a mine, Dwelt a

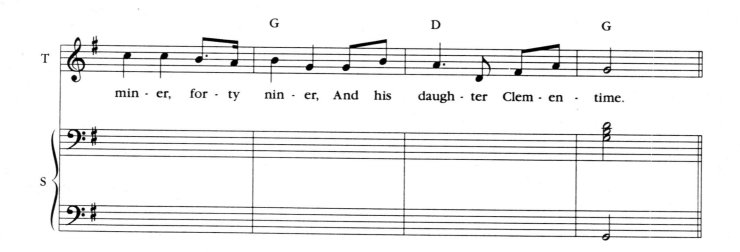

min - er, for - ty nin - er, And his daugh - ter Clem - en - tine.

Chorus

Oh, my dar - ling, Oh, my dar - ling, Oh, my dar - ling Clem - en - tine! You are

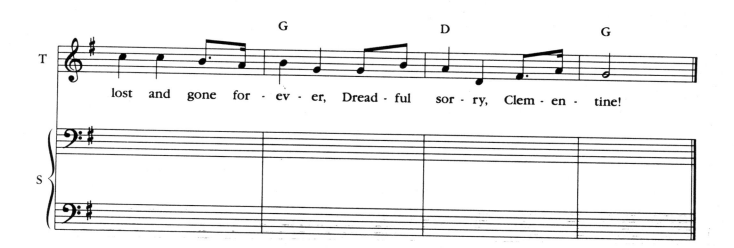

lost and gone for - ev - er, Dread - ful sor - ry, Clem - en - tine!

Other possibilities for voicing the RH include:

or:

GO LITTLE BOAT

(Miss 1917)

words by **P. G. Wodehouse**
music by **Jerome Kern**
arr. Lyke

Go lit - tle boat, se - rene - ly glid - ing;

O - ver the sil - ver wa - ter rid - ing.

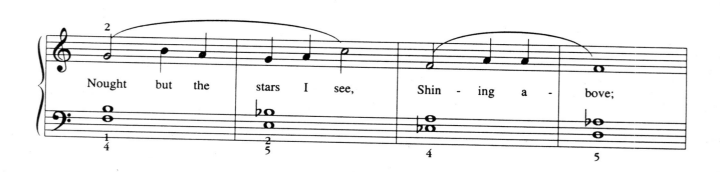

Nought but the stars I see, Shin - ing a - bove;

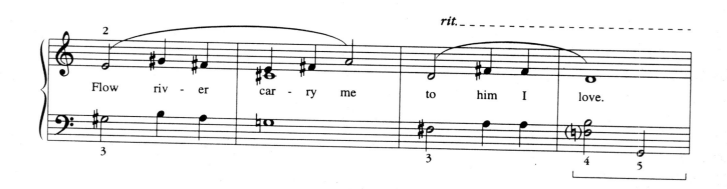

Flow riv - er car - ry me to him I love.

a tempo

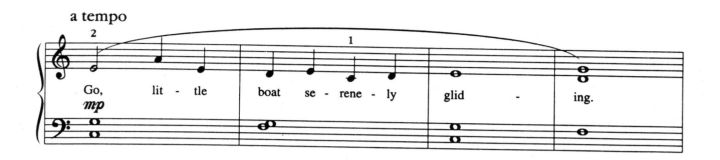

Go, lit - tle boat se - rene - ly glid - ing.

Love at the helm your course is guid - ing.

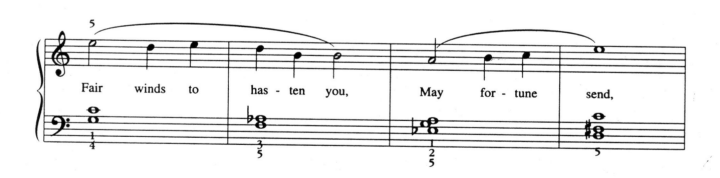

Fair winds to has - ten you, May for - tune send,

till I come safe to jour - ney's end.

BY THE BEAUTIFUL SEA

words by **Harold R. Atteridge**
music by **Harry Carroll**
arr. **Lyke**

By the sea, by the sea, by the beau - ti - ful sea, you and

I, you and I, Oh! how hap - py we'll be,

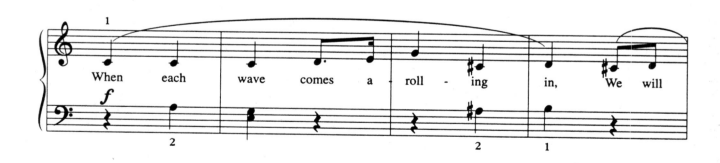

When each wave comes a roll - ing in, We will

duck or swim, And we'll float and fool a - round the wa - ter,

O - ver and un - der, and then up for air,_____ Pa is

rich, Ma is rich, So now what do we care?_____

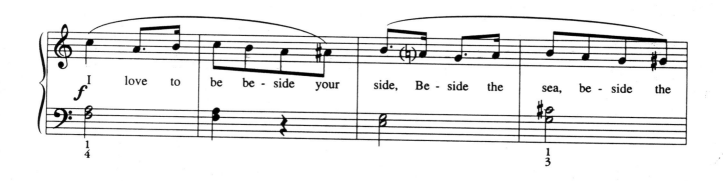

I love to be be - side your side, Be - side the sea, be - side the

sea - side, By the beau - ti - ful sea._____

108

Ensemble

In the two duets, *Blue Mood* and *In a Minor Mood,* both primo and secondo may be played by students. Again ♫ should be treated as ♩ ♪ so that the eighths "swing".

BLUE MOOD
Secondo

Céline Bussières-Lessard

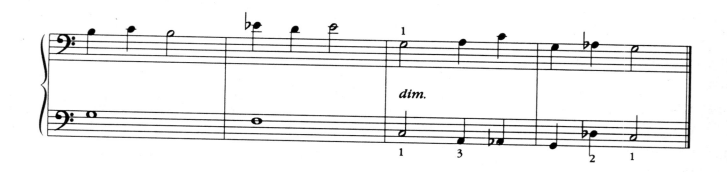

BLUE MOOD

Primo

Céline Bussières-Lessard

IN A MINOR MOOD

Secondo

Céline Bussières-Lessard

IN A MINOR MOOD

Primo

Céline Bussières-Lessard

CLEOPATTERER

(Leave It To Jane)

Secondo—Teacher

music by **Jerome Kern**

arr. Lyke

LH staccato simile

CLEOPATTERER
(Leave It To Jane)
Primo—Student

music by **Jerome Kern**
arr. Lyke

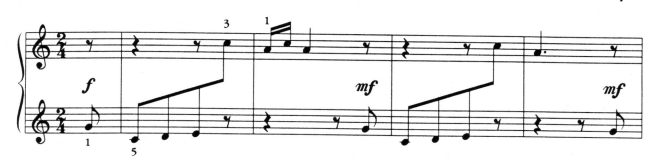

VIVE LA COMPAGNIE

Secondo–Teacher

College Song
arr. Heitler and Lyke

With spirit

VIVE LA COMPAGNIE

Primo—Student

College Song
arr. Heitler and Lyke

Repertoire

Find pentachord and triad outlines. Also find an inverted E major chord which is outlined.

ADAGIO

Gürlitt

MINUET

Johann Krieger

BURLESKE

from Leopold Mozart's
"Notebook for Wolfgang"

MAJOR—MINOR MIX

Caramia

MISSING YOU

Caramia

A LITTLE JOKE

Kabalevsky

BLUES

Ben Blozan

Minor Pentachord Review

Build the minor pentachords indicated below. Draw letters on the correct keys, as shown in number one.

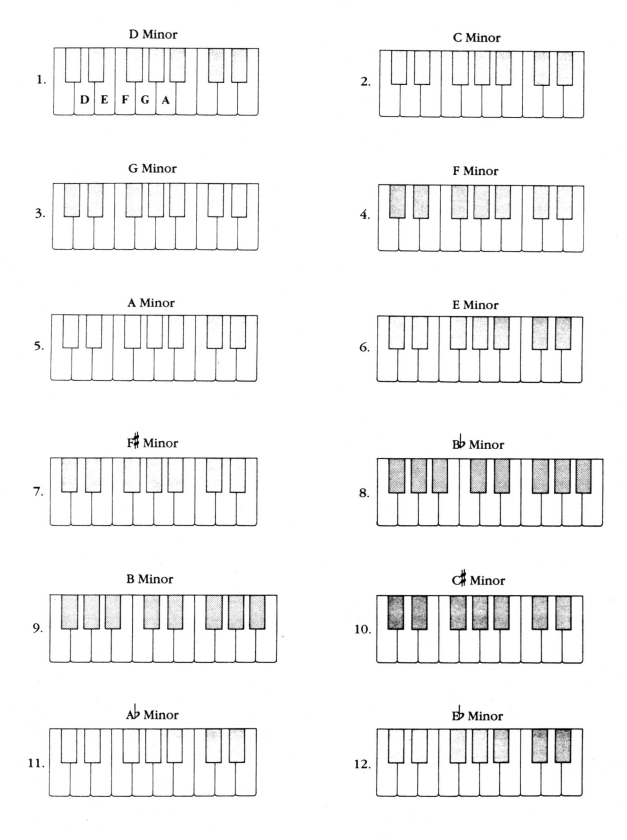

Identify the following minor key signatures. Determine the major key signatures, then count down one and a half steps, or a minor 3rd.

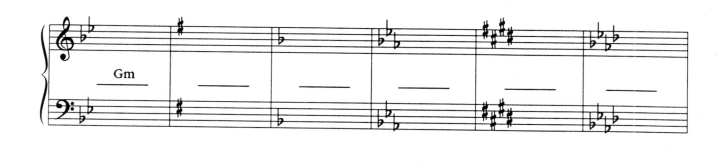

Triad Review

From letter name chord symbols, notate the following triads using proper accidentals.

Ear Training Activities

(1) Your teacher will play several pentachords. Some will be major and others will be minor. Distinguish from the sound which are major and which are minor. Here might be a typical sequence: Em, Cmaj, B♭ maj, Fm, Dm. Students need only respond to each as "major" or "minor." (2) Your teacher will play several triads. Some will be major and other will be minor. Identify each as major or minor. Here might be a typical sequence: Cm, Emaj, Fmaj, Bm, Gm. Students need only respond to each as a major or minor triad. (3) Your teacher will play several short melodic patterns within a minor pentachord. The key will be given. Listen to these patterns twice and play back with rhythmic and melodic accuracy. Here might be some typical examples:

Improvising

Continue the suggested beginning of the piece in A minor, ⁶⁄₈ meter. Improvise at least twelve more bars. Try to include a contrasting phrase.

Use major and minor root position triads in the RH. End with the triad used at the beginning.

Limit the melody to tones of the E minor pentachord. End on E minor.

Technic

The following exercises emphasize minor pentachords and minor triads. Transpose exercises two and three chromatically through all minor keys.

Right Hand Alone

Left Hand Alone

VARIATION ON A GURLITT STUDY

Alexander

Transpose to selected minor keys

SUGGESTED QUIZ TOPICS — CHAPTER FOUR

1. Play minor pentachords on any keynote, followed by the minor triad on that keynote.

2. Demonstrate harmonization skill in minor keys by playing any lead sheet realization on page 93.

3. Show an understanding of $\frac{6}{8}$ meter and the feel of "two" (♩. ♩.) by playing either *French Folk Song* on page 95.

4. Demonstrate skill with sixteenth notes by playing any song arrangement from pages 100 or 101.

5. Chord the accompaniment to *Clementine* (pages 102–103) using any of the three starting chord patterns.

6. Play one American song arrangement from pages 104–107.

7. Play one duet part from the duet selections on pages 108–115.

8. Play one solo from pages 116–122.

CHAPTER 5 — Chord Inversion, The Dominant Seventh Chord, The Subdominant Chord, Harmonization, Triplets, Syncopation, Repertoire, Theory and Technic

AMERICAN FOLK SONG

Read the melody of *American Folk Song* and notice the chord outline of the tonic in bars 1 and 2. All the tones of C major are present, but the lowest tone is G. Block this chord. The fifth is on the bottom, root in the middle and third on top. The rearrangement of these tones results in a *chord inversion*. Study the chord in root position, first inversion and second inversion as shown below. Any triad may be inverted.

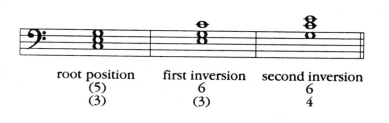

root position   first inversion   second inversion
(5)   6   6
(3)   (3)   4

$\genfrac{}{}{0pt}{}{(5)}{(3)}$	— The bass tone is the root of the triad.
$\genfrac{}{}{0pt}{}{6}{(3)}$	— The bass tone is the third of the triad.
$\genfrac{}{}{0pt}{}{6}{4}$	— The bass tone is the fifth of the triad.

A kind of musical shorthand flourished in the seventeenth and the first half of the eighteenth centuries known as *figured bass*, or *thorough bass*. In this system, chords were represented by Arabic numerals which related the upper tones to the bass. These numbers delineated intervals above the bass tone, but not necessarily in vertical order. In figured bass playing, the numbers in parentheses were taken for granted, and not included. An absence of numerals meant the triad was in fundamental position (root in the bass).

In folk and popular music another system is used. The letter names of the chord appear above the melody line. Often letter names will appear with a slash mark. The letter following the slash tells what note should be in the bass (the lowest note).

C   C/E   C/G   G/D   Am/C   Dm/A

AMERICAN FOLK SONG

In the same song, study the chord outline in bars 5 and 6. The dominant (V) triad is outlined and one more third is added to the chord. This makes a *dominant seventh* chord (root, third, fifth plus seventh). All seventh chords contain four tones. This most important of these are the root, third and seventh. The fifth is often omitted. The V and V^7 chords have a strong tendency to move to the tonic (I) chord.

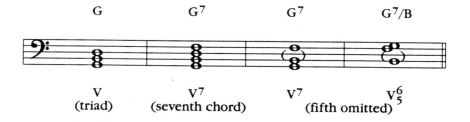

Voice Leading

To avoid awkward sounds (and awkward fingerings) it is important that tones of successive chords move to the nearest tones, or to common tones. Study the two examples below to understand how inversions help chord voices to move smoothly.

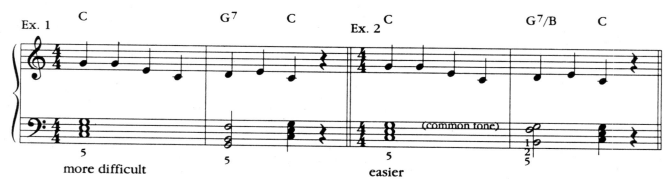

Chord Progression I V^6_5 I

Practice the chord progression below. Transpose it to other major keys. When moving from I to V^6_5: leave the thumb on the common tone, finger 2 is placed on the fourth step of the major pentachord (up 1/2 step) and finger five moves down a 1/2 step (to the seventh step of the scale). Add chord symbols.

continue

Melodies to Harmonize with I and V$_5^6$

Harmonize the following melodies with the tonic chord and the first inversion of the dominant seventh chord. Melodies 1 and 2 use block chords as a LH style. Label each chord (above the melody) with letter name symbols. Fill in the blank LH measures.

SKIP TO MY LOU

American

GERMAN CAROL

Melody no. 3 is enhanced with a LH broken chord accompaniment. Again, label each chord and fill in all blank measures according to the example.

BRITISH FOLK TUNE

BRITISH FOLK TUNE

Triads on Scale Degrees

Triads may be built on all scale degrees. These chords are called *diatonic* chords. Diatonic means *in the key* of the scale. These chords also have various qualities: major, minor, and diminished (like minor but contains a lowered fifth). Practice building these chords in C major. Play them, identify them verbally, then move on to the next chord. Transpose this study to a few more keys (F, G, D etc.) Notice that I, IV and V are major; II, III, and VI are minor; VII is diminished. This will be the case in all major keys.

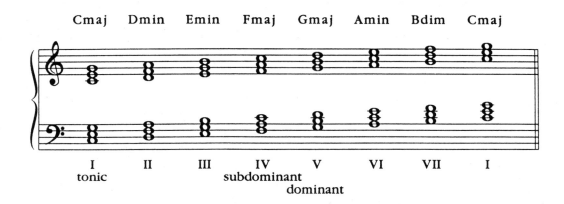

The Subdominant (IV) Chord in Major Keys

The subdominant chord is built on the fourth scale degree. It most often moves to the tonic (I) or dominant (V). The three most used chords in music are the I, IV and V chords; therefore these chords are known as *primary*. Chords built on other tones of the scale (II, III, VI etc.) are known as *secondary* chords.

Melody Analysis

Analyze the chord outlines in the melody which follows. Three measures have complete outlines. Circle these measures. Melody tones which don't fit in the chord are called *non-chord* tones. Some non-chord tones used in the melody below include *passing tones* (p.t.) and the *suspension* (suspended over from a previous harmony). Other non-chord tones will be identified later.

NORWEGIAN MELODY

As we learned when dealing with V^7 in root position as opposed to V^7 in first inversion (V_5^6), inversions help the hand assume a more comfortable position. In LH style harmonization, it is easier to move from I to V_5^6 and return to I. I-V-I is less smooth. The same is true when I moves to IV or IV moves to I, or to V_5^6. Study the examples below.

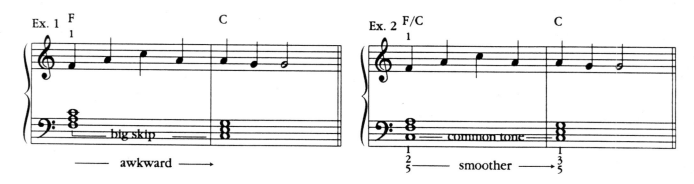

Harmonization

Using LH block style, harmonize the complete Norwegian Melody using the chord symbols above the melody (this is a lead line). Notate the LH harmony.

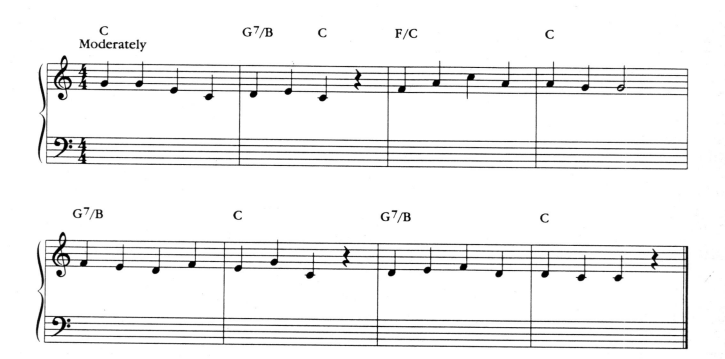

I IV⁶₄ I Chord Pattern

Practice the chord pattern which follows. Transpose it to several keys.

continue

Before learning to play *When The Saints Go Marching In*, analyze the harmony in the LH. Use letter name symbols and slashes. Find chord melody outlines in the melody. Another non-chord tone appears in the melody. Measure 4 contains an *upper neighboring tone* (u.n.).

WHEN THE SAINTS GO MARCHING IN

When chord tones are prominent in the melody and when they repeat as in bars one and two, plus five and six, it is not necessary to double that tone in the LH.

SOLDIER, SOLDIER

Anglo

Chord Progressions

Practice the following progressions in the keys suggested. Block LH, then RH and finally play in piano style, e.g., single bass tones (roots) with the chord in the RH. Note the two ways to practice the piano style example.

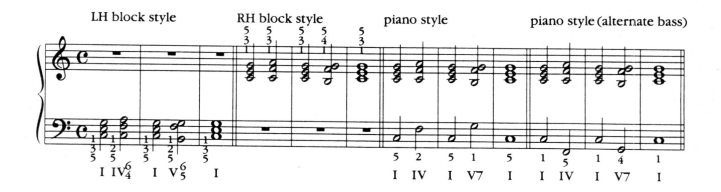

Accompanying

Play the chordal accompaniment (S) while your teacher (T) plays the melody to *German Folk Song*. Observe fingering and dynamics carefully.

GERMAN FOLK SONG

Transpose to G

Triplets

An eighth note triplet 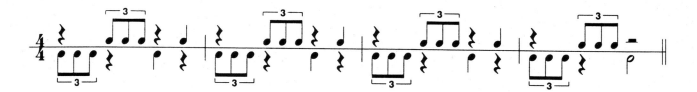 fills the time of one quarter note. Practice tapping and clapping the following rhythmic pattern.

Triad Triplet Study

Practice the following study which outlines triads in triplet figures. Transpose this study to B♭ and D.

FRENCH FOLK SONG

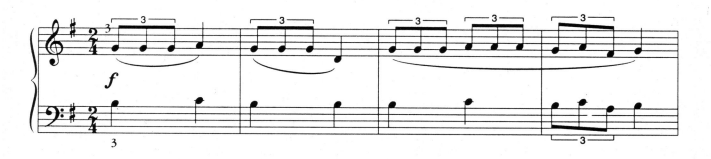

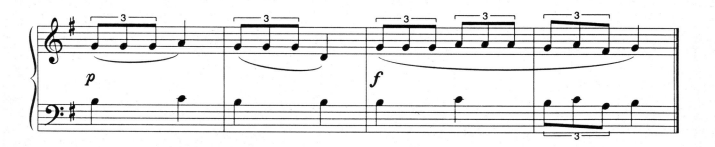

Music for Reading

The reading studies which follow focus on new elements introduced in this chapter: V^7, V^6_5, IV, IV^6_4, inverted chords and triplets. As in the previous chapters, tap the rhythms, identify keys and chord outlines in the melody, analyze the accompaniment and determine any chord inversions. Try to grasp details beyond just notes and rhythm, e.g., touch, dynamics, tempo and fingering.

FOR HE'S A JOLLY GOOD FELLOW

D.C. al fine

Transpose to G

⌢ *fermanta* – A sign for a pause. Hold the note at least twice its value before proceeding to the next note.

WELSH MELODY

Transpose to Gm

ON TOP OF OLD SMOKEY

SHE'LL BE COMIN' 'ROUND THE MOUNTAIN

American

Transpose to F

VOLGA BOAT SONG

Russian

Transpose to Dm

Clef Changes

To avoid excessive leger lines and make reading easier, changes of clef become necessary. The change of clef will be signaled in the preceding measure (see bars 4-5, 8-9 and 12-18 in the LH).

THE GLOW WORM

P. Lincke

Shine lit-tle glow worm glim-mer, glim-mer Shine lit-tle glow worm glim-mer, glim-mer

Lead us, lest too far we wan-der, Love's sweet voice is call-ing yon-der,

Shine lit-tle glow worm glim-mer, glim-mer Shine lit-tle glow worm glim-mer, glim-mer

light the path be - low, a - bove and lead us on to love.

140

Syncopation

When a weak beat, or a weak part of a beat is stressed, *syncopation* occurs. In measures 1, 2, 5, 6, 9, 10, and 13 of *Do, Lord*, the normally weak second beat receives more emphasis because a long note (𝅗𝅥) falls on that beat. Tap the RH rhythm before playing.

DO, LORD

Gospel Song
arr. Lyke

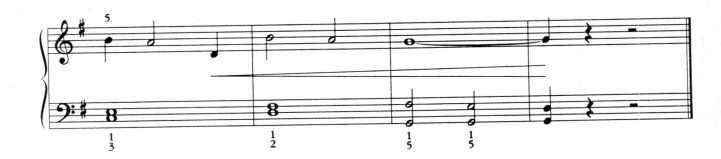

HELLO MA BABY

words by **Ida Emerson**
music by **Joe Howard**
arr. Lyke

YOU'RE HERE AND I'M HERE
(The Marriage Market)

words by **Harry B. Smith**
music by **Jerome Kern**
arr. Lyke

You're here and I'm here, so what do we care?___ The time and

place do not count, It's the one who is there;___ Now all I

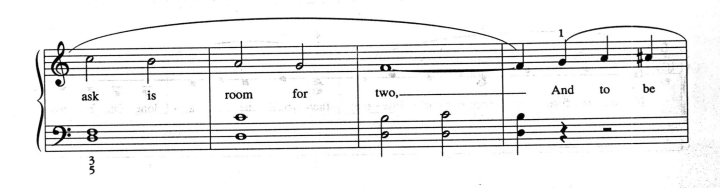

ask is room for two,___ And to be

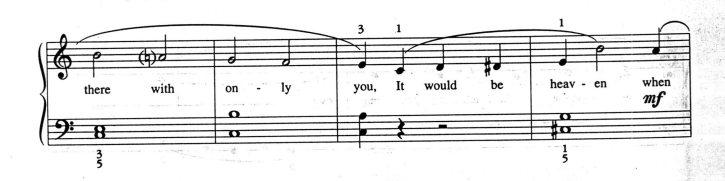

there with on-ly you, It would be heav-en when

two hearts are true hearts, like yours and mine, The skies are

fair ev'-ry where, and the sun seems to shine, And now the

wide world seems a lit-tle co-sy cor-ner, For

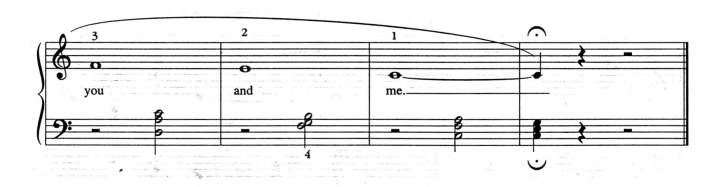

you and me.

TILL THE CLOUDS ROLL BY
(Oh, Boy)

words by **P. G. Wodehouse**
music by **Jerome Kern**
arr. Lyke

Oh, the rain comes a pit-ter pat-ter, And I'd

like to be safe in bed. Skies are

weep-ing while the world is sleep-ing Troub-le heap-ing

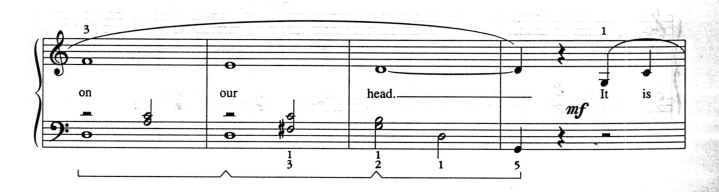

on our head. It is

Ensemble

FOR NORMAN
Secondo

Tony Caramia

Ensemble

D.S. *(dal segno)* – from the sign 𝄋 – Repeat the composition from the sign 𝄋.
⊕ (coda sign) – Disregard the first time through; the second time, skip from this sign ⊕ to the coda mark ⊕ near the end of the composition

FOR NORMAN

Secondo

Tony Caramia

Primo

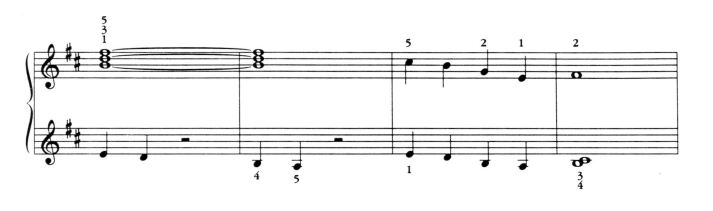

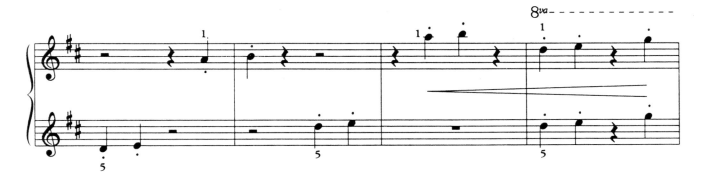

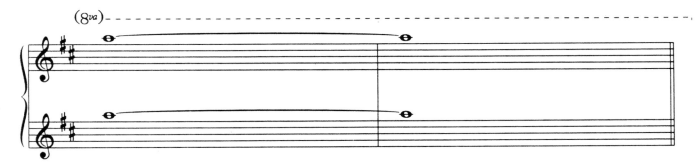

D.S. al ⊕

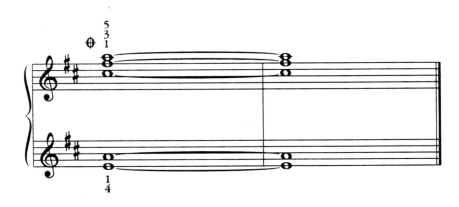

LEAVE IT TO JANE

Secondo–Teacher

words by **P. G. Wodehouse**
music by **Jerome Kern**
arr. Lyke

LEAVE IT TO JANE

Primo—Student

words by **P. G. Wodehouse**
music by **Jerome Kern**
arr. Lyke

Moderately bright

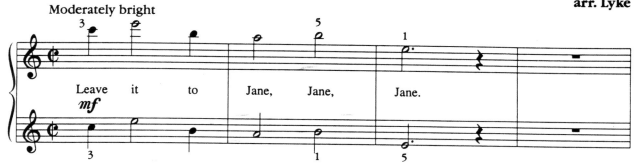

Leave it to Jane, Jane, Jane.

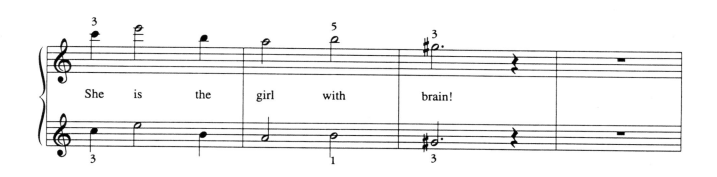

She is the girl with brain!

No prob - lem you can wish on her gives her a strain;

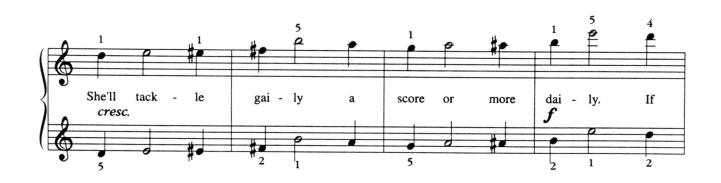

She'll tack - le gai - ly a score or more dai - ly. If

Secondo

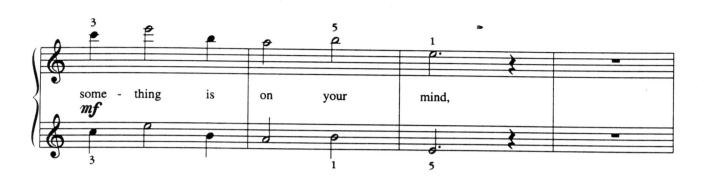

some - thing   is   on   your   mind,

mf

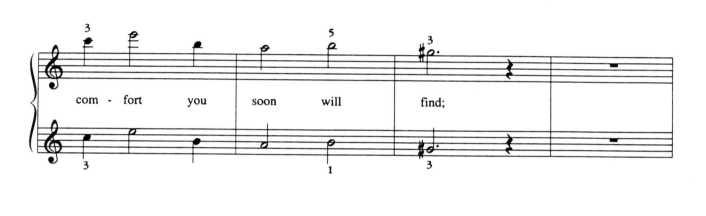

com - fort   you   soon   will   find;

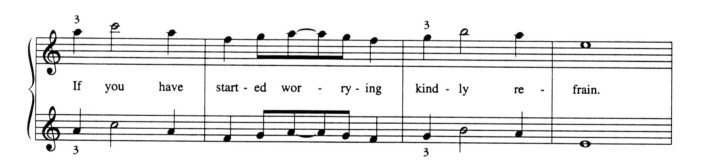

If   you   have   start - ed   wor - ry - ing   kind - ly   re - frain.

And   just   hand   o - ver   the   whole   thing   to   Jane.____

f

Repertoire

Practice suggestions: block LH chords, label each with letter name and denote any inversions. Isolate the RH in bars 5-7 to grasp the change of position. Work for balance between the hands, RH singing out, LH accompanying.

MELODY

Köhler

In *Minuet,* analyze the harmony. Find the tonic, subdominant and dominant chords and label them with both Roman numerals and letter name symbols.

MINUET

Mozart

DANCE

Ben Blozan

D.C. al fine

IN A PENSIVE MOOD

Caramia

OUTLINES

Lyke

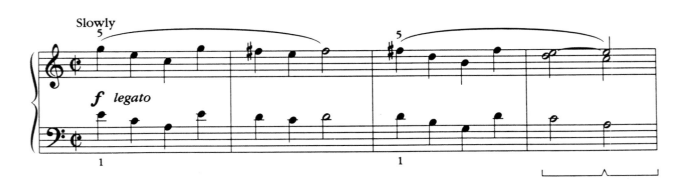

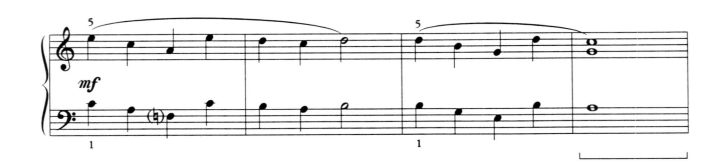

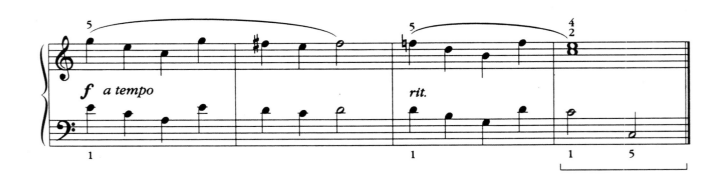

PIRATE'S SONG

Ben Blozan

Theory Review

Identify both major and relative minor key signatures below. For minor, count down one and one-half steps, or a minor 3rd.

Build major pentachords on the keynotes given below.
Formula: whole step, whole step, half step, whole step.

Build minor pentachords on the keynotes given below.
Formula: whole step, half step, whole step, whole step.

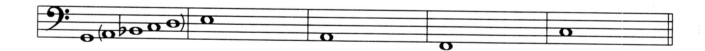

Build major triads from the given note.

Build minor triads from the given note.

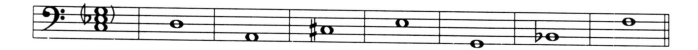

Tonic, Subdominant, Dominant Seventh

Complete the following patterns. Move to the closest voice.

Complete the following I V$^6_5$ I patterns.

I   V$^6_5$ I   I   V$^6_5$ I   I   V$^6_5$ I   I   V$^6_5$ I

Identify the triads below. Use slashes to give the correct bass note.

F/C

162

Ear Training

(1) After a tonic chord is sounded, you will hear a series of four chords, consisting of either I, IV, or V. Identify the sequence correctly.

Ex. (T)

(S)   I–I–IV–V

(2) After hearing rhythmic patterns such as the following tapped, notate them.

Ex.

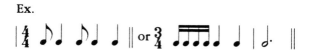

(3) Identify triads as being in root position, first inversion or second inversion. Your teacher will play them broken and blocked.

Ex.

Improvising

In no. 1, use the LH ostinato from *Pirate's Song* and improvise a melody in the RH Dm pentachord. In no. 2, complete the final four bars using the LH waltz pattern. In no. 3, follow the instructions given.

Technic: Fingering Concepts for Major Scales

The following chart outlines all fingering patterns for major and minor scales. Play scalar patterns by dividing each individual scale into its logical fingering clusters of three and four groups (123–1234). See Appendix B for a thorough presentation of all major scales. Start to learn scales systematically as you proceed through this book.

Fingering Chart	
Major Scale Fingerings	Minor Scale Fingerings (Harmonic)
Right-Hand White Note Scales C D E G A B: 123-1234-123-1234-5 F: 1234-123-1234-123-4	Right-Hand White Note Scales Same as major scale fingerings
Left-Hand White Note Scales C D E F G A: 5-4321-321-4321-321 B: 4-321-4321-321-4321	Left-Hand White Note Scales Same as major scale fingerings
Left-Hand Alternate Fingerings D: 21-4321-321-4321-21 F: 321-4321-321-4321-3 G: 321-321-4321-321-43 A: 21-321-4321-321-432	No minor alternate fingerings
Right-Hand Black Note Scales D♭: 23-1234-123-1234-12 E♭: 3-1234-123-1234-123 G♭: 234-123-1234-123-12 A♭: 34-123-1234-123-123 B♭: 4-123-1234-123-1234	Right-Hand Black Note Scales E♭: same as E♭ major G♯: same as A♭ major B♭: same as B♭ major C♯: 34-123-1234-123-123 F♯: 34-123-1234-123-123
Left-Hand Black Note Scales D♭ E♭ A♭ B♭: 321-4321-321-4321-3 G♭: 4321-321-4321-321-4	Left-Hand Black Note Scales C: same as D major G: same as A major F: same as G major E♭: 21-4321-321-4321-32 B♭: 21-321-4321-321-432

164

Held Notes

Articulate fingers clearly while holding down the thumb or fifth finger.

Right Hand Alone

Repeat in C minor

Left Hand Alone

Repeat in C minor

SUGGESTED QUIZ TOPICS — CHAPTER FIVE

1. Block any major or minor triad in root position, first inversion and second inversion; be able to block the dominant seventh in root position and first inversion (omitting the 5th).

2. Block triads on the scale degrees of the following keys: C, D, E, F, G, A, B, E♭, A♭. As you block, identify each by letter name and quality.

3. Play the chord progression (LH) I–IV$^6_4$–I–V$^6_5$–I in any key.

4. Play the chord progression I–IV–I–V^7–I in four voices (bass in LH, chord in RH). Play this pattern in selected major keys.

5. Demonstrate an understanding of syncopation by playing *Hello Ma Baby* (page 141).

6. Play one Jerome Kern song from the American Song Repertoire section (pages 142-145).

7. Play one ensemble piece from the Ensemble Section (pages 146-153).

8. Play one solo from the Repertoire section (pages 154-159).

9. Demonstrate an understanding of scale fingering principles (page 163 and Appendix B).

6 Secondary Chords, The Pentatonic, Whole Tone and Chromatic Scales, Harmonization, Repertoire, Theory and Technic

Secondary Chords

We have analyzed, played and used the primary chords, I, IV and V in various ways. Secondary chords, II, III and VI *substitute* for primary chords. Secondary chords are also known as subordinate triads. Study the bracketed secondary chords. All are minor in quality.

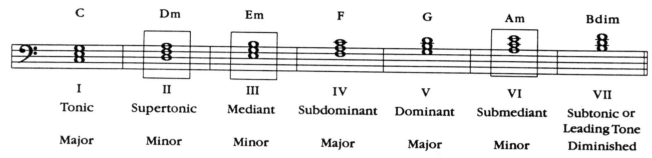

The normal progression of these chords is a movement to IV or V and ultimately to I.

Progression No. 1

Play this progression and study the voice leading. Only one voice changes in the RH from I to VI and IV to II. Then a typical cadence (closing chords) of I_4^6–V^7–I ends the progression. Minor triads are often symbolized in lower case lettering.

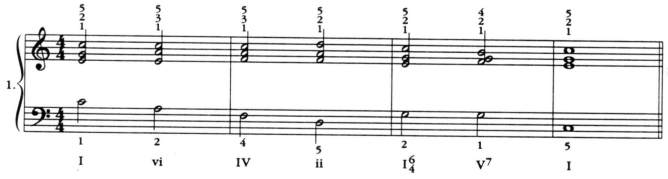

Transpose to several keys

Progression No. 2

This harmonization of the descending scale line highlights the III chord. The cadence, II^6–I_4^6–V^7–I is a typical classical formula.

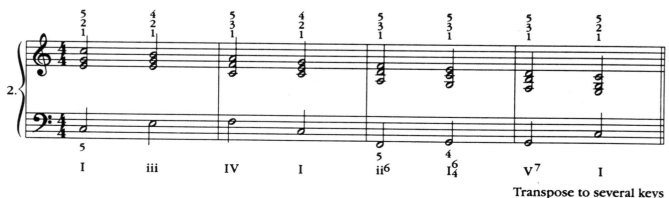

Transpose to several keys

Music for Reading and Analysis

Analyze the primary and secondary chords used to harmonize the following melodies. Label these chords and indicate any inversions. Circle all secondary chords. The II chord is most often found in first inversion (II^6).

DANISH FOLK SONG

ENGLISH FOLK SONG

DANISH FOLK SONG

ENGLISH FOLK SONG

Harmonization

Harmonize melodies 1–4 with an appropriate LH style (block, broken chord, waltz, etc.). Notate the harmonies indicated by the chord symbols. Suggested beginnings are offered.

MELODY

Paisiello

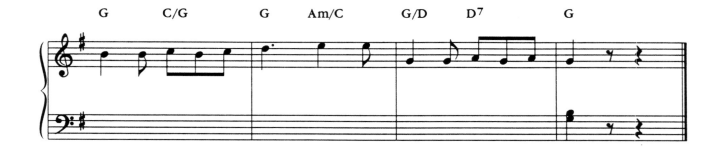

GERMAN FOLK SONG

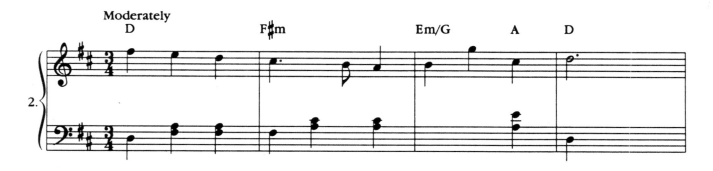

ITALIAN FOLK SONG

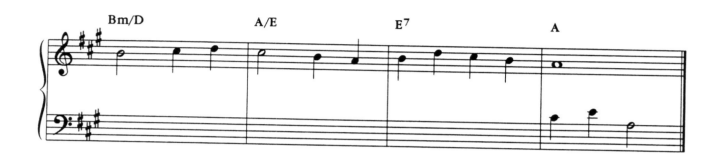

I'M TRAMPING

American

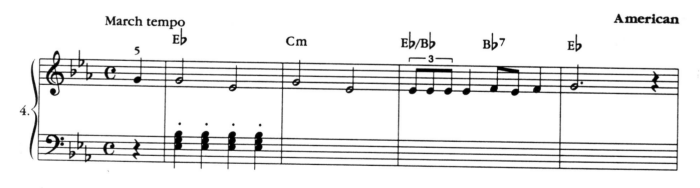

Chording Accompaniments—Piano Style

Before reading the accompaniments, practice the preliminary chord patterns. Label all chords with letter name and quality, and identify any inversions. A new chord, the Am^7, is formed by adding another third to the Am triad.

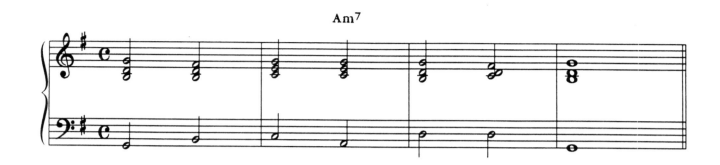

FINNISH MELODY

VIVE L'AMOUR

With spirit

The Pentatonic Scale

Observe the keyboard diagram below which shows two patterns for the pentatonic scale. The pentatonic scale is a primitive scale of five consecutive tones within the octave. The scale corresponds to the black keys on the keyboard. The pentatonic scale can begin on any black key.

Pentatonic Scale
(Two patterns for the right hand)

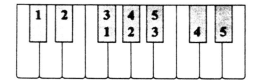

The pentatonic scale may be played on white keys also. Using the top numbers above, slide the hand right and play D E G A B. Using the lower numbers, slide the hand left and play F G A C D.

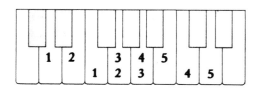

SOURWOOD MOUNTAIN

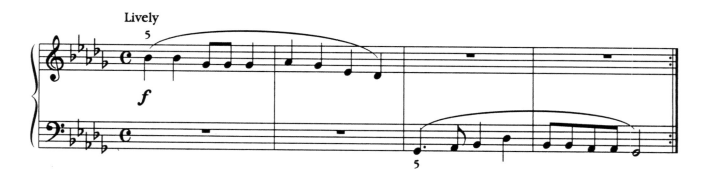

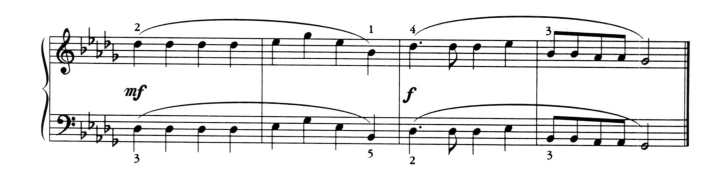

The Whole Tone Scale

Another scale which twentieth century composers, such as Debussy, have used in various ways is the whole tone scale. The whole tone scale is a six-note scale (hexatonic). Study the diagram below which shows the two possibilities for dividing the twelve tones into two patterns.

Use of the whole tone scale provides an "atmospheric" effect when the pedal is employed. Play the simple study below. Begin to improvise whole tone melodies using a LH *ostinato* (recurring bass figure) as shown in the study.

WHOLE TONE STUDY

Lyke

The Chromatic Scale

A chromatic (from chroma - color) scale consists of the twelve pitches within the octave, e.g., the pitches of all the black and white keys. It is seldom used in its entirety. Examine the chromatic scale beginning on C.

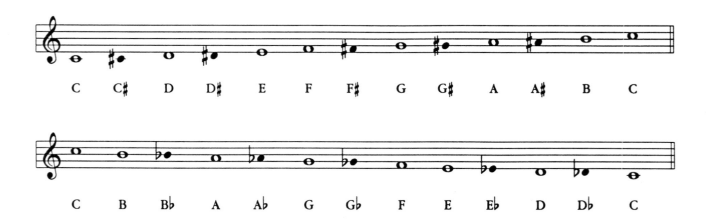

Fingering for the chromatic scale is given in the *Technic* section at the end of this chapter.

CHROMATIC SCALE STUDY

Lyke

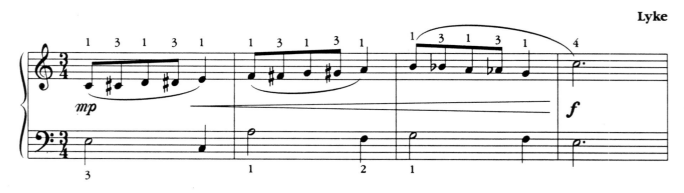

Music for Reading

The following arrangements stress 1) secondary chords and 2) pentatonic melodies and chromatic passages. Follow the normal reading routine (tapping the rhythm, analyzing melodic patterns, identifying familiar harmonies, etc.). Then set a tempo and begin to read with *no stops*.

LEAVE HER JOHNNY
(LH Style)

Shantey

GERMAN FOLK SONG
(Piano Style)

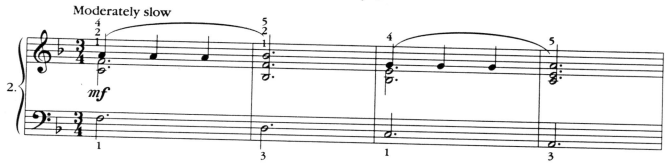

FRENCH FOLK SONG
(Piano Style)

LOCH LOMAND

Scottish

CROATIAN MELODY

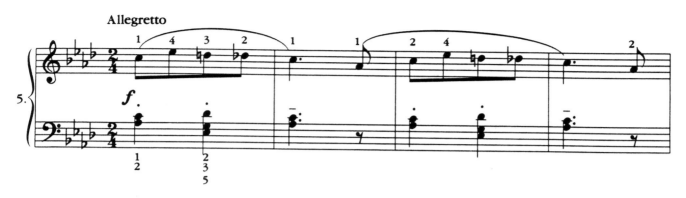

IN GOOD OLD COLONY TIMES

American

Transpose to F

STOP, STOP, STOP
(Come Over and Love Me Some More)

words and music by
Irving Berlin
arr. Lyke

PRETTY BABY

words by **Gus Kahn**
music by **Egbert Van Alstyne**
arr. Lyke

Ev-'ry bod-y loves a ba-by that's why I'm in love with you Pret-ty Ba-by, Pret-ty Ba-by; And I'd

like to be your sis-ter, bro-ther, dad and moth-er too, Pret-ty Ba-by, Pret-ty Ba-by. Won't you

come and let me rock you in my cra-dle of love, And we'll cud-dle all the time.___ Oh! I

want a lov-in' Ba-by and it might as well be you, Pret-ty Ba-by of mine.___ Ev'ry mine.___

WHEN I LOST YOU

words and music by
Irving Berlin
arr. Heitler and Lyke

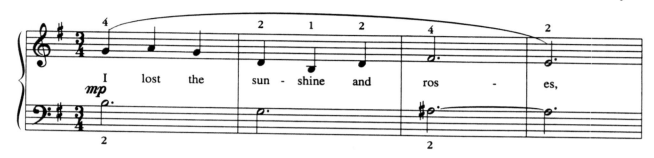

I lost the sun - shine and ros - es,

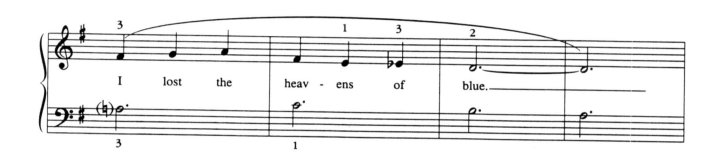

I lost the heav - ens of blue.

I lost the beau - ti - ful rain - bow,

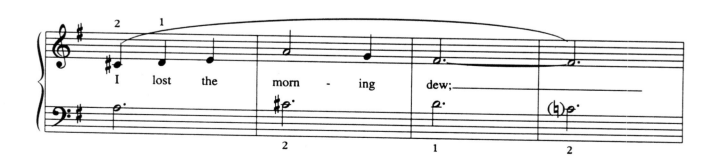

I lost the morn - ing dew;

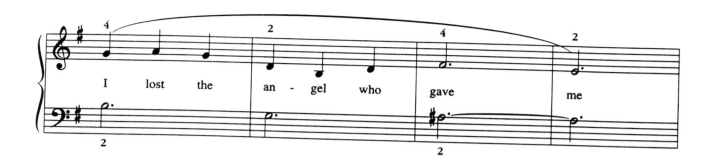

I lost the an - gel who gave me

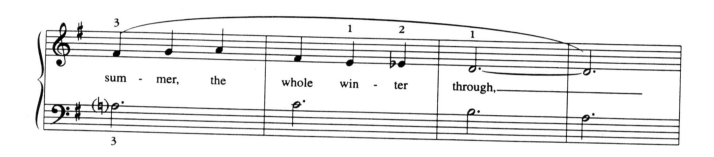

sum - mer, the whole win - ter through,

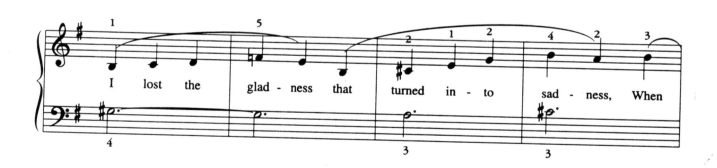

I lost the glad - ness that turned in - to sad - ness, When

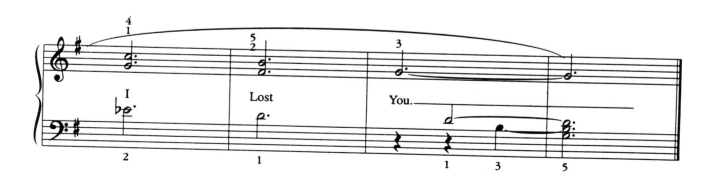

I Lost You.

DREAMING

Secondo—Teacher or Student

Céline Bussières-Lessard

D.C. al fine

DREAMING

Primo—Student

Céline Bussières-Lessard

D.C. al fine

AH! VOUS DIRAISE-JE MAMAN

Secondo—Teacher

Céline Bussières-Lessard

- - whole tone scale - -

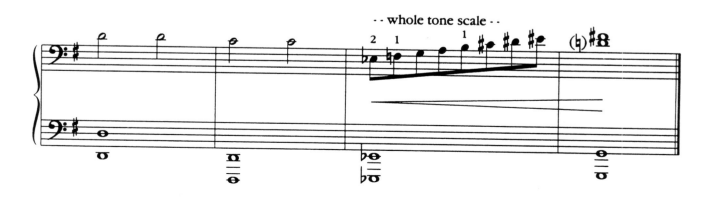

AH! VOUS DIRAISE-JE MAMAN

Primo—Student

Céline Bussières-Lessard

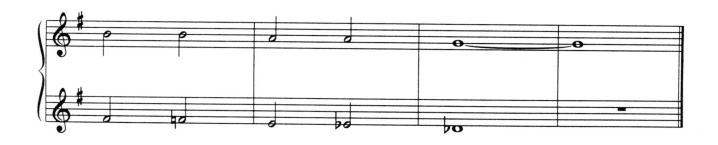

GERMAN DANCE
(Secondary Chords)

Beethoven

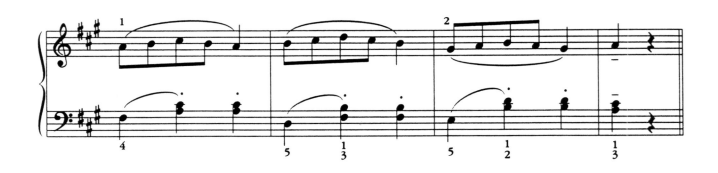

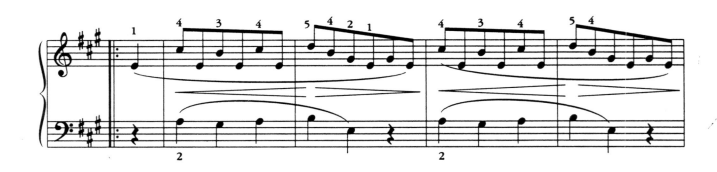

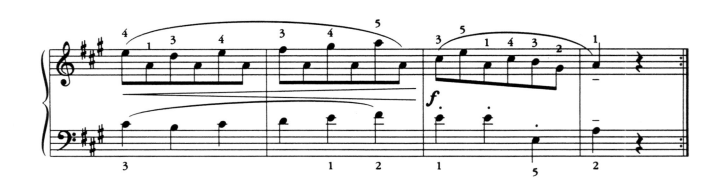

ALLEGRO
(Primary Chords, Supertonic)

Schytte

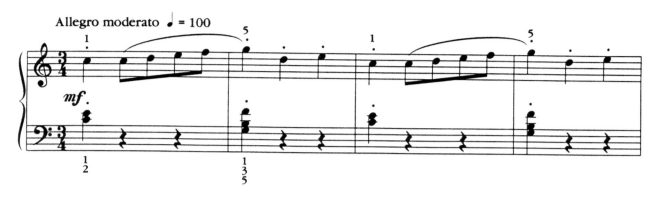

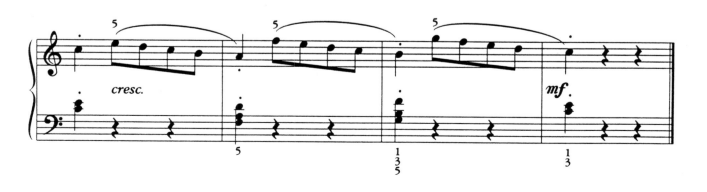

ANDANTE
(Chromatics)

Caramia

SONATINA

(Triplet Review)

W. Duncombe

SPOOKS
(Whole Tones)

Caramia

Slowly, mysteriously

WITH APOLOGIES, GEORGE!

(Pentatonic)

Caramia

192

Theory Review

Build supertonic (II) chords in the following keys. Notate root position and both inversions as shown in the example. Label each chord with Roman numerals (beneath) and letter names with appropriate slashes (above).

Gm   Gm/B♭   Gm/D

Follow the instructions above with submediant (VI) chords.

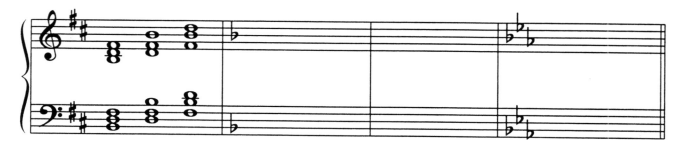

Follow the same instructions for mediant (III) chords.

Fill in the **RH** missing notes for this familiar chord progression. Add letter name symbols.

I   VI   IV   II   I$^6_4$ V^7 I

Ear Training

As your teacher plays brief chord patterns, identify each pattern by Roman numerals or letter name symbols. Starting chord will be given.

Ex. Teacher:

Student:

$I–II^6–V^7–I$ or
$C–Dm/F–G^7–C$

Improvising

Continue the following beginnings. Expand each to *at least* two four-bar phrases.

White key pentatonic, LH ostinato.

Black key pentatonic, LH ostinato.

Whole tone, LH ostinato.

Technic: The Chromatic Scale in Contrary Motion

A chromatic scale divides the octave into twelve half-steps. The alternate fingerings will work well in rapid tempi. Notice that by starting a third apart, the fingerings become mirrored and they are, therefore, the same for each hand. Memorize one set of fingerings.

SUGGESTED QUIZ TOPICS — CHAPTER SIX

1. Play the chord progressions involving secondary chords on page 165 in at least three keys.

2. Demonstrate a knowledge of applying secondary chords to harmonizations by playing one realization from pages 168–169.

3. Build pentatonic scales on any black key. Immediately transpose them to the closest white keys.

4. Build a whole tone scale on C and on C♯.

5. Play a chromatic scale in the RH ascending from middle C to C an octave higher. Descend back to middle C.

6. Transpose *German Folk Song* (page 175) to G.

7. Play one American Song from the American Song Repertoire section, pages 178–181.

8. Play one duet from the Ensemble section, pages 182–185.

9. Play one solo from the Repertoire section, pages 186–191.

10. Demonstrate a knowledge of chromatic scale fingering by playing a chromatic scale in the RH; ascend from E above middle C to E an octave higher, then descend. With the LH, descend from middle C to an octave below middle C, then ascend.

7 The Dominant of the Dominant, The Minor Scale, Modes, Harmonization, Repertoire, Theory and Technic

Study the D^7 chord in bars 2 and 6. This chord is not in the key of C, but embellishes the next chord V^7(G) which is in the key. The D^7 chord has a root a 4th below or a 5th above G^7. In this key, the D^7 is termed a *dominant of the dominant* (V^7 of V^7).

THAT'S WHERE MY MONEY GOES

American

Secondary Dominants

Any triad may be preceded by its own dominant; these are termed secondary dominants. These chromatic chords add color and enrich the harmony. The most common secondary dominant is $V^{(7)}$ of $V^{(7)}$. Study scale degree triads embellished by their respective dominants. The dominants are built a *fourth* below the root of each triad.

| I | V^7 | I | ii | V^7 of ii | ii | iii | V^7 of iii | iii | IV | V^7 of IV | IV | V | V^7 of V | V |

Chord Pattern: I–IV–V^7/V^7–V^7–I

Practice the familiar I–IV–V^7 chords with the added V^7 of V^7. Transpose this pattern to F and G.

| I | IV | V^7/V | V^7 | I |

Transpose to F and G

Reading and Analysis

Read and study the following arrangements which make use of the V⁷ of V⁷ or V of V. Notice how often the dominant of the dominant precedes a cadence on the $V^{(7)}$ chord, a *half cadence*. The cadence from V to I is called an *authentic cadence*. A IV–I cadence is termed *plagal* (as in the "Amen" of hymns).

FLOW GENTLY, SWEET AFTON

Hume

Transpose to G

THE ASH GROVE

Welsh

Harmonization

Harmonize melodies 1 and 2 with LH styles as suggested. Melodies 3–5 will be in a piano style setting.

Preliminary to No.1

Preliminary to No. 2

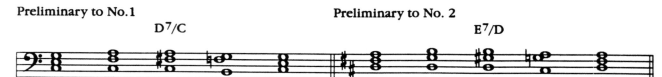

COLLEGE SONG

American

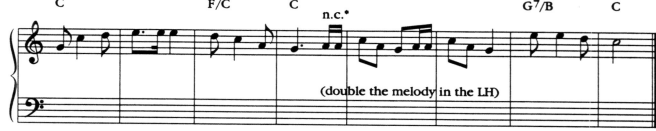

(double the melody in the LH)

* n.c. = no chords

AUSTRIAN CAROL

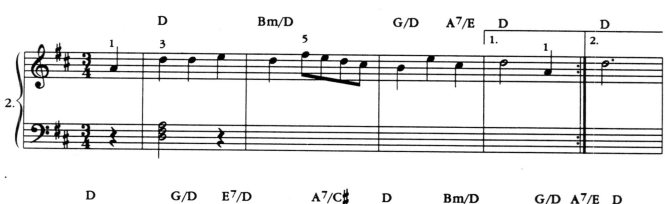

THE MUFFIN MAN
(Two voices in the RH)

British

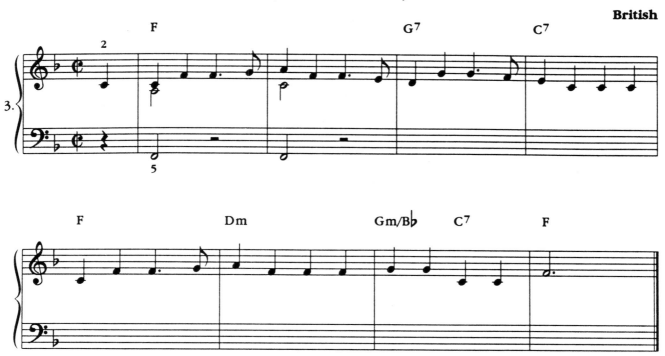

Fill in two voices beneath the melody note. Only one voice beneath the melody note is necessary at the downbeat of bar 5 and bar 6.

HOME ON THE RANGE
CHORUS

American

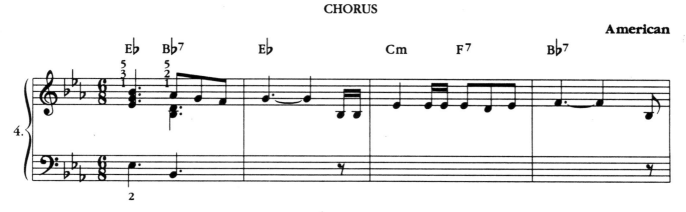

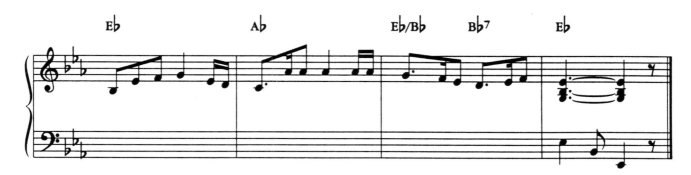

JINGLE BELLS
CHORUS

Pierpont

Chording an Accompaniment

Before playing the accompaniment to *Cockles and Mussels,* practice the chord pattern. Label all chords in the pattern *and* in the accompaniment. Identify any inversions.

COCKLES AND MUSSELS

Slowly   Irish

202

The Minor Scale

There are three forms of the minor scale: 1) *natural* 2) *melodic* and 3) *harmonc*. Study all three built on A.

A Natural Minor

A Melodic Minor

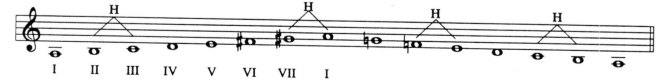

A Harmonic Minor (most common)

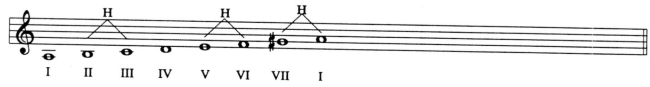

*H = 1/2 step

Minor Key Signatures

All minor scales share a major scale key signature. This may be found by counting up one whole and one half step from the minor keynote. C major is the *relative major* key of A minor. And A minor is the *relative minor* key of C major. To find the relative minor from the major scale keynote, count down one and a half steps. Study the whole step/half step arrangement of all three minor scales.

Parallel Scales

Play the A major scale which follows. Then play the A harmonic minor scale, contrasting it to the major scale. You will notice that in the harmonic minor scale, the 3rd and 6th degrees are lowered one half step. The 7th (raised a half step in the harmonic minor) is the same as in A major.

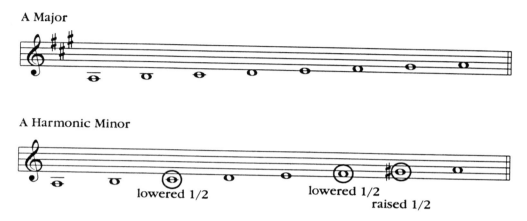

Study Piece

Determine the minor key of *Two Guitars* (key of one flat, count down 1 1/2 steps from the major keynote). The raised leading tone C♯ tells us we are in harmonic minor. The tonic and subdominant chords in a minor key will be minor in quality. Analyze the chords.

TWO GUITARS

Slovakian

* sixteenth rest 𝄾 = ♪

Music for Reading and Analysis

Before playing each excerpt, determine the key and harmonies. What form of minor scale is used in each example?

RUSSIAN FOLK SONG

Arr. Beethoven

DANCE

Haydn

Harmonization of Minor Melodies

Harmonize the following melodies in minor keys. Melodies 1 and 2 will use a LH style; melodies 3 and 4 will use piano style. In minor, the tonic and subdominant chords will be minor. The dominant and dominant seventh will be exactly the same as in the parallel scale. Notate your arrangement.

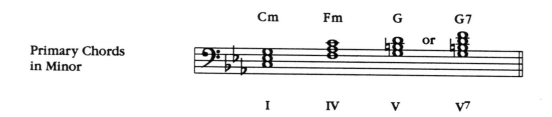

GO DOWN MOSES

Spiritual

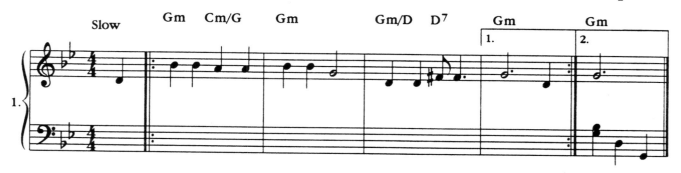

CZECH FOLK SONG

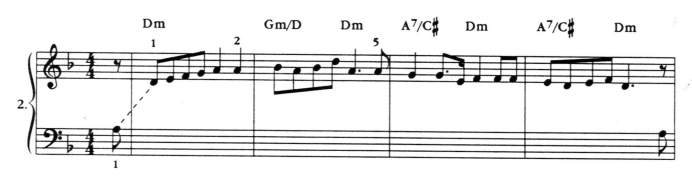

ITALIAN FOLK SONG
(Two voices in RH)

SPANISH FOLK SONG

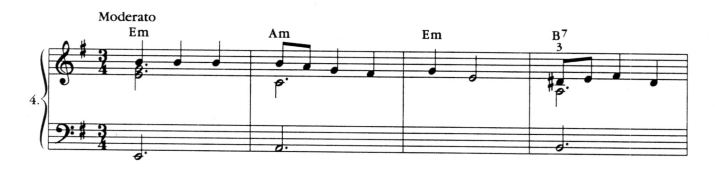

Chording an Accompaniment in Minor

Practice the minor chord pattern below until the fingering feels comfortable.

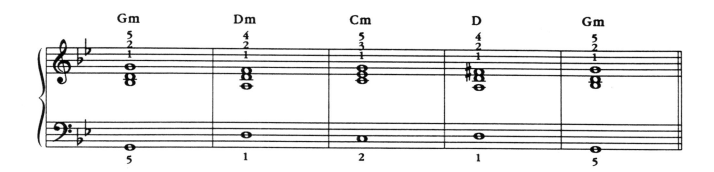

Notate the incomplete measures in the accompaniment.

MEADOWLANDS

Russian

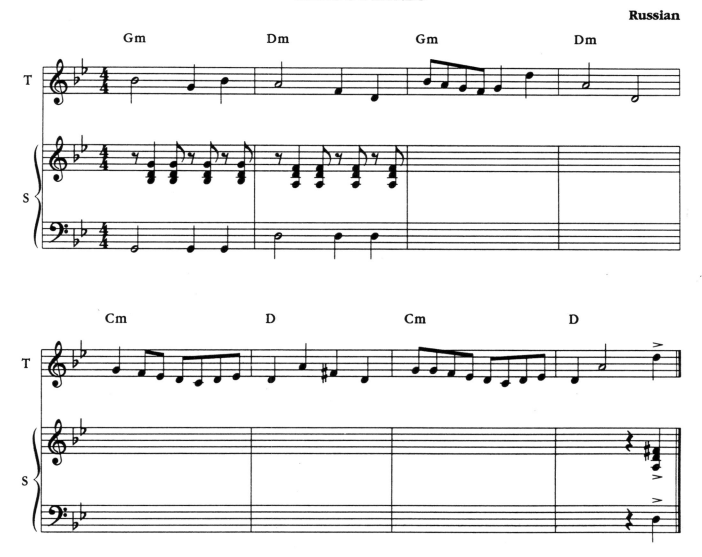

Modes

We have already explored major and minor scales, or *modes*. And we have had experience with other modes such as the pentatonic and whole-tone. The Church modes are centuries old and have been used in folk song melody (especially Eastern Europe) and in plainsong (Gregorian chant). The untransposed modes can be played on the white keys of the piano with no accidentals. Two of the modes, Ionian and Aeolian, are constructed the same as the major and natural minor scales. Twentieth century composers have used the church modes to get away from traditional major and minor sound. Study the white key modes below. Play and listen to them. Analyze how each differs from the familiar major and minor.

UNTRANSPOSED MODES

Ionian mode – same as major.

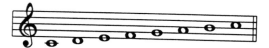

Lydian mode – resembles major except for the raised fourth.

Dorian mode – resembles minor except for the raised sixth.

Mixolydian mode – resembles major except for the lowered seventh.

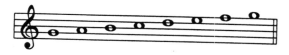

Phyrygian mode – resembles natural minor except for the lowered second.

Aeolian mode – same as natural minor.

Locrian mode – a theoretic mode which is infrequently used.

Transposing the Modes

The modes may be transposed to any key other than the white note form. Always think of the relationship the white key modes have with C. For example, D dorian takes the key signature of C, a major second below D. Therefore, E dorian would take the key signature of D—two sharps. E dorian would be spelled: E, F sharp, G, A, B, C sharp, D and E. The interval relationship is always maintained. For phrygian, use the key signature of a third below the tonic; for lydian, a fourth below, for mixolydian, a fifth below (or fourth above); for aeolian, a minor third above, and for locrian, a half-step above.

When a piece appears to be modal, and the tonal center has been determined, the mode can be quickly analyzed. For example, if the tonal center appears to be F, and the key signature has five flats, the mode is obviously phrygian, since D flat is a major third below F.

Music for Reading and Analysis

The sea chantey below makes use of the dorian mode. The two most used chords are Dm and Cmaj. Learn this piece to experience the flavor of modal melody and harmony.

THE DRUNKEN SAILOR

Chantey

Two Modal Melodies to Harmonize

Harmonize the following melodies according to the suggested style.

SCARBOROUGH FAIR
(Dorian)

British

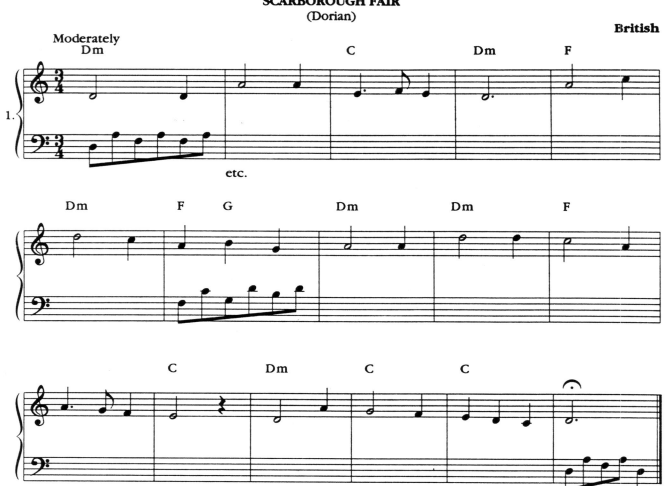

JOHNNY HAS GONE FOR A SOLDIER
(Aeolian)

Irish

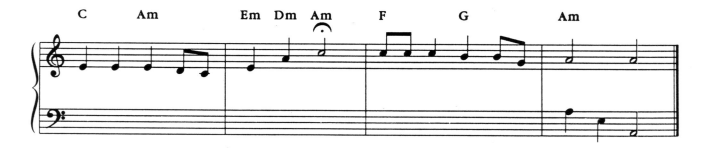

More Modal Music for Reading and Analysis

Can you determine the mode used in *When Johnny Comes Marching Home?*

WHEN JOHNNY COMES MARCHING HOME

American
arr. Lyke

Here is a piece in lydian mode. The scale resembles G major but the fourth scale degree is raised throughout. Compare this scale to the white key lydian mode, built on F.

SHARP FOUR

Frackenpohl

PAPER DOLL

words and music by
Johnny Black
arr. Lyke

THE SIREN'S SONG*

(Leave it to Jane)

words by **P. G. Wodehouse**
music by **Jerome Kern**
arr. Lyke

Come to us we've wait-ed so long for you, Ev - 'ry day we'll make a new song for you,

Come, come, to us we love you so.

Leave be-hind the world and its fret - ting and we will give you rest and for-get - ing; So

sang the si - rens a - ges and a - ges a - go.

*The sirens in this song refer to mermaids.

KISS ME, MY HONEY, KISS ME

words and music by
Ted Snyder and Irving Berlin
arr. Lyke

Kiss me, my hon-ey, Kiss me, And say you'll

miss me as I'll miss you;

Love me, my hon-ey, love me, Like stars a-

bove me, say you'll be true while a-way ev-'ry day, I'll be think-ing of you

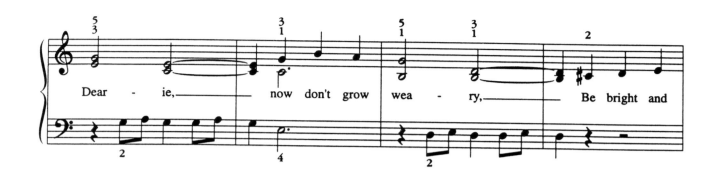

Dear - ie,_____ now don't grow wea - ry,_____ Be bright and

cheer - y,_____ my hon - ey do,_____

so dear,_____ be - fore I go, dear,_____ come here and

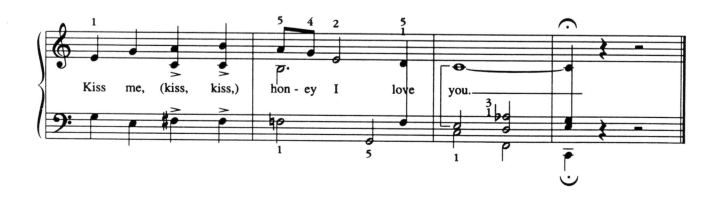

Kiss me, (kiss, kiss,) hon - ey I love you._____

Ensemble

TANGO ARGENTINO

Secondo–Teacher or Student

Céline Bussières-Lessard

TANGO ARGENTINO
Primo–Student or Teacher

Céline Bussières-Lessard

MARCH
Secondo–Teacher or Student

Céline Bussières-Lessard

Allegro

fine

D.C. al fine

MARCH

Primo–Student or Teacher

Céline Bussières-Lessard

D.C. al fine

Repertoire

What minor scale does Bartók use in *Dialogue*?

DIALOGUE

Bartók

PLAINTIVE MELODY

Ben Blozan

224

SONG

Spindler

In *Adagio*, the scale is similar to the A natural minor, but the sixth degree is raised (F#). What mode is used?

ADAGIO

Bartók

MIXING MINOR AND MAJOR

Schytte

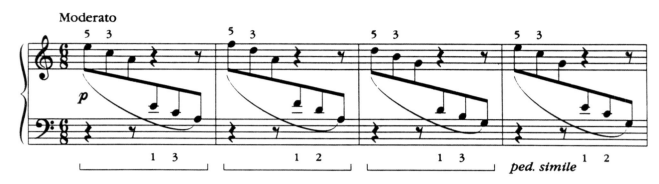

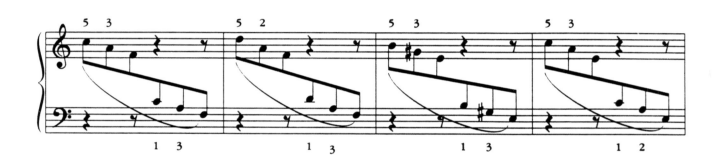

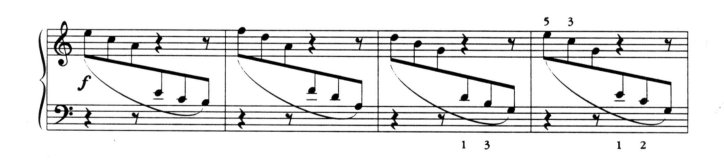

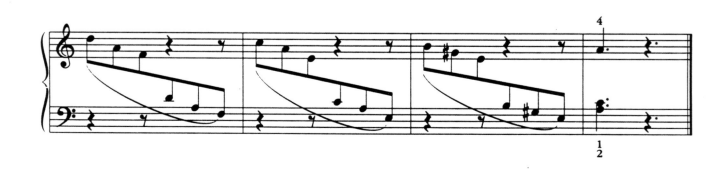

WALTZ

Kabalevsky

PERPETUAL MOTION

Lyke

Theory Review

Build natural minor scales on the given tones and add the proper accidentals. The third of the tonic minor chord will give you the key signature.

Build harmonic minor scales on the given tones. Remember to raise the seventh degree one half step.

Fill in the missing tones in the following two progressions. Move to the closest voice.

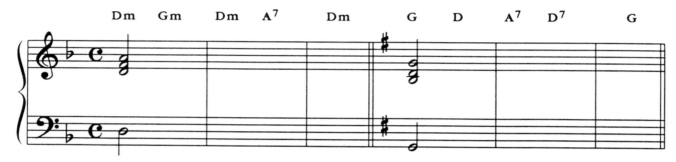

Build modes on the given tones and add proper accidentals. Review the material on modal transposition and key signatures found in this chapter.

C Dorian

A Phrygian

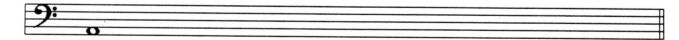

D Lydian

F Mixolydian

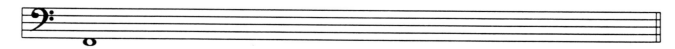

Ear Training

1) Identify the various forms of the minor scale (natural/aeolian mode, melodic and harmonic) played by your teacher.

2) Identify short minor chord sequences or progressions played by your teacher.

Ex. 1   Ex. 2

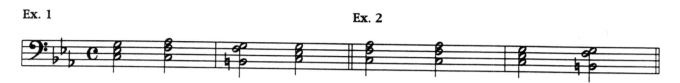

Improvising

Use this G lydian LH pattern as a basis for RH melody improvisation.

Use this LH figure from the Bartók *Adagio* as an ostinato. Improvise a melody using tones of the A minor pentachord.

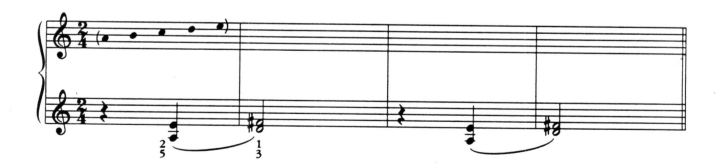

Technic

Continue the systematic study of scales (and arpeggios) in Appendix B. Play the white key minor scales of C, D, E, G, A and B using the same fingerings as the parallel major. Play the harmonic form. Consult the fingering chart at the end of Chapter Five.

SUGGESTED QUIZ TOPICS — CHAPTER SEVEN

1. Play the chord progression I-IV-V^7 of V-V^7-I in five or six keys. (See the beginning of Chapter Seven.)

2. Demonstrate harmonization skill using V^7 of V by playing any piano style arrangement on pages 199 and 200.

3. Be able to build the natural, melodic and harmonic minor scales on any tone.

4. Demonstrate harmonization skill in the minor mode by playing either arrangement on page 206.

5. Show the ability to "chord" an accompaniment by playing either *Cockles and Mussels* (page 201) or *Meadowlands* (page 207).

6. Know any white key form of the various modes. Be able to compare the mode to a major or minor scale which differs slightly. (ex.: D dorian is similar to D natural minor, but the 6th scale degree is raised one half step.)

7. Play one American song from the American Song Repertoire section, pages 214-217.

8. Play one duet from the Ensemble section, pages 218-221.

9. Play one solo from the Repertoire section, pages 222-229.

10. Compose a short piece using one of the improvisational ideas at the end of this chapter.

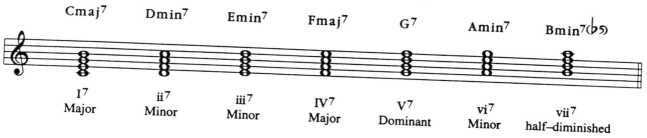

CHAPTER 8

Seventh Chords, Introduction to the Jazz Idiom, Modulating Patterns (to Closely Related Keys), Chording, Repertoire, Theory and Technic

Seventh Chords on Scale Degrees

Study the quality of the various seventh chords built on major scale degrees shown below. Block seventh chords on scale degrees in selected major keys and identify the quality of each chord. Say the Roman numeral, then letter name and quality as you build each chord on scale degrees of each new key.

Transpose to F, E, G and D

Seventh Chord Qualities

We have studied triads and their various qualities (major, minor, augmented and diminished). Similarly, seventh chords may be identified by various qualities. Examine the qualities of seventh chords built on the diatonic scale above. Below, the five main types of seventh chords are shown. Build these on various tones. After building the major seventh, note that *only one tone* changes in the order of given chords.

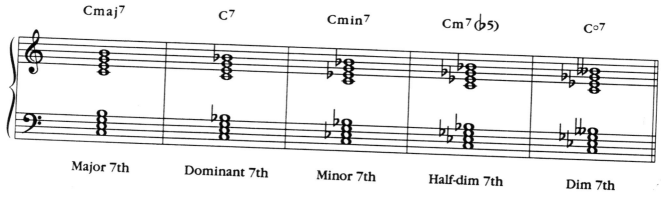

Two Chord Patterns

Practice these two chord patterns in a few selected keys. It is important to observe the bass line: up a fourth, down a fifth, up a fourth, etc. Develop a *feel* for the right hand fingering.

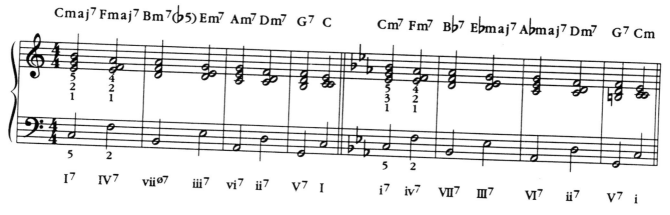

234

Music for Reading and Analysis

Seventh Heaven uses LH voicings of seventh chords with a step-wise movement. These voicings are termed *close position.* Analyze all chords (including quality) in the LH. Pedal the chords, taking a new pedal with each chord change.

SEVENTH HEAVEN

Caramia

Voicing Seventh Chords Between the Hands (open position)

Sevenths are spread between the hands in *Pattern In Color*. Analyze all chords. Place symbols above the melody. Pedal each chord change. Notice how the rhythmic figure ♪♪ ♩ ♩ | ♪♪ ♩ | unifies this composition.

PATTERN IN COLOR

Andante ♩ = 72

Alec Wilder

From *Twelve Mosaics for Piano.* Permission to reprint from Theodore Presser Company.

II⁷–V⁷–I

The first progression in the Wilder composition is a standard progression in jazz. Complete the fill in's below and in other selected keys.

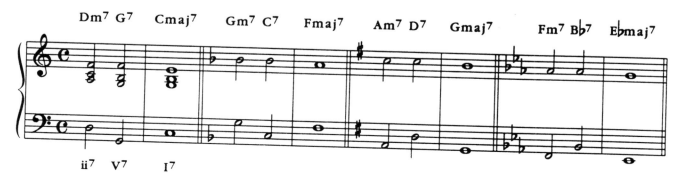

Dm⁷ G⁷ Cmaj⁷ Gm⁷ C⁷ Fmaj⁷ Am⁷ D⁷ Gmaj⁷ Fm⁷ B♭⁷ E♭maj⁷

ii⁷ V⁷ I⁷

Blues

The blues form originated early in jazz history. Features of the blues include a twelve bar structure with a progression normally employing four bars of tonic, two bars of subdominant, two bars of tonic, two bars of dominant and two bars of tonic. Variations of this pattern exist. Other features include the use of *blue* notes in the melody. In this compositon the blue notes include B♭ (lowered 7th of the C scale) and E♭ (lowered 7th of the F scale).

SLOW BLUES

Caramia

BLUE WALTZ

Caramia

Rags

Piano rags preceded jazz style piano. Well known writers of rags include Scott Joplin, Jelly Roll Morton and Eubie Blake. A significant feature of many rags is the syncopated figure: ♪ ♩ ♪ (used in the composition below).

A RAG

Moderately

Caramia

fine

D.C. al fine

238

Popular Songs

The arrangements which follow use *seventh chords*, and *dominant sevenths* outside the key to arrive at cadence points which represent a temporary shift to a new key center. Analyze the chords. Jazz musicians love to improvise on the chord structures or "changes" of popular songs.

FOR ME AND MY GAL

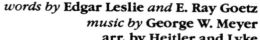

words by **Edgar Leslie** *and* **E. Ray Goetz**
music by **George W. Meyer**
arr. by Heitler and Lyke

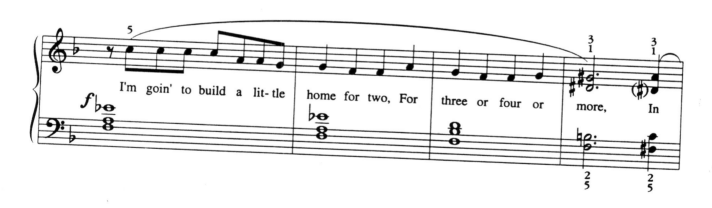

YOU SAID SOMETHING

(Have a Heart)

words *by* **Jerome Kern** *and* **P. G. Wodehouse**
music *by* **Jerome Kern**
arr. Lyke

You said some-thing when you said you loved me,

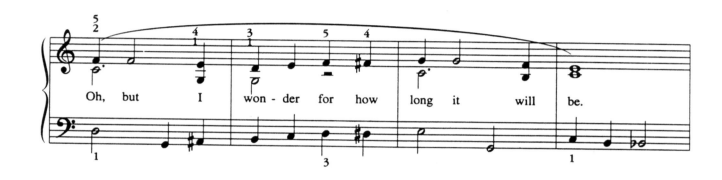

Oh, but I won-der for how long it will be.

If you find some-day, you've al-tered your mind

I'd be for-giv-ing, but sim-ply could not go on liv-ing!

Girls much pret - tier you will meet by the score,

will you re - gret you nev - er met them be - fore?

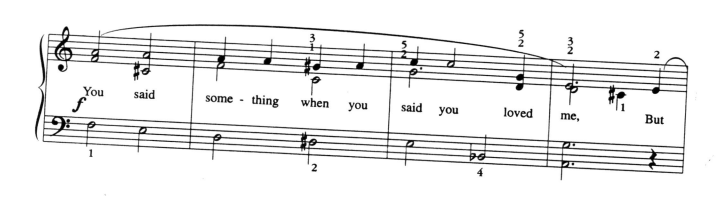

You said some - thing when you said you loved me, But

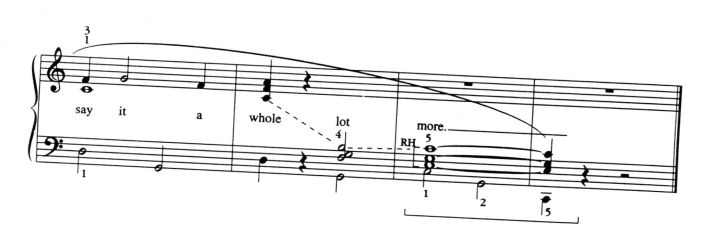

say it a whole lot more.

SMILES

(Melody in LH)

words by **J. Will Callahan**
music by **Lee G. Roberts**
arr. Lyke

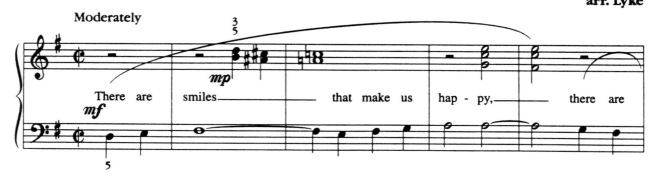

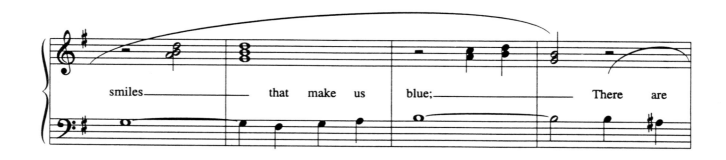

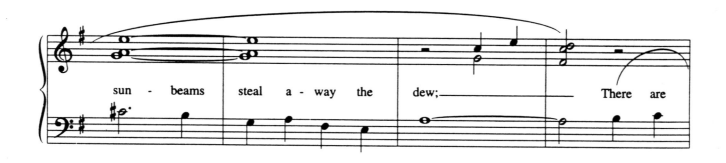

smiles that have a ten - der mean - ing_____ that the

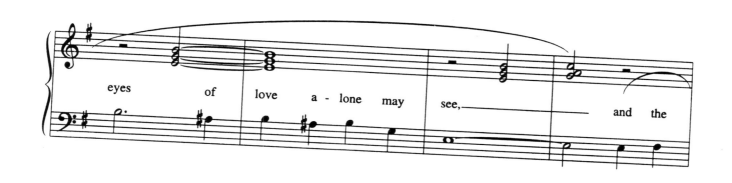

eyes of love a - lone may see,_____ and the

smiles that fill my life with sun - shine_____ are the

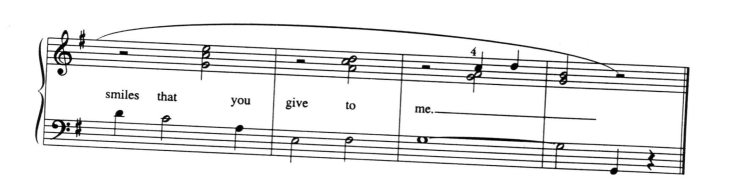

smiles that you give to me._____

POOR BUTTERFLY

words by **John Golden**
music by **Raymond Hubbell**
arr. **Lyke**

Slowly with expression

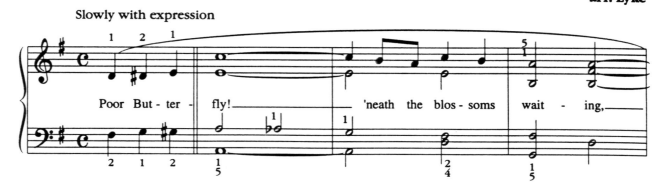

Poor But - ter - fly!_____ 'neath the blos - soms wait - ing,_____

Poor But - ter - fly!_____ For she loved him so._____

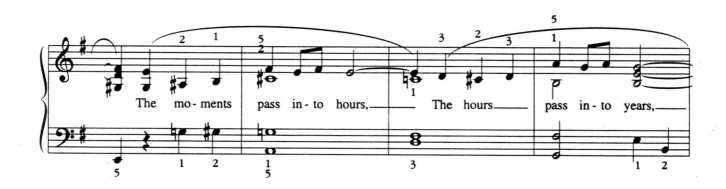

The mo - ments pass in - to hours,_____ The hours_____ pass in - to years,_____

And as she smiles through her tears,_____ She mur - mers low,_____

The moon and I know that he be faith - ful,

I'm sure he come to me bye and bye.

But if he don't come back, then I nev - er sigh or cry,

I just mus' die. Poor But - ter - fly.

(BACK HOME AGAIN IN)
INDIANA

words by **Ballard MacDonald**
music by **James F. Hanley**
arr. **Lyke**

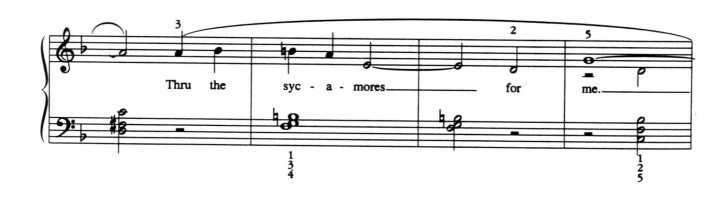

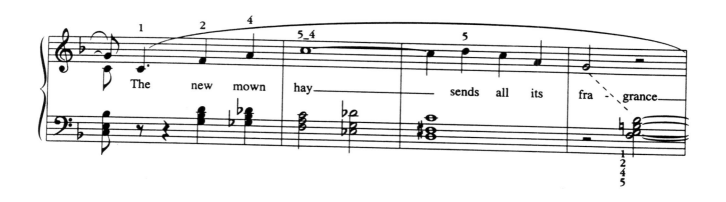
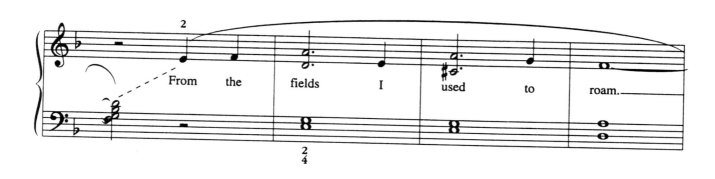
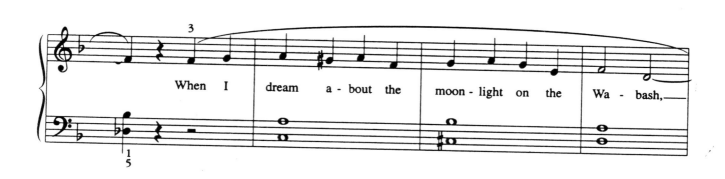

248

Modulation to the Dominant Key

In the excerpt below, note how Pleyel achieves a temporary shift to the dominant key at the double bar. The D minor harmony in bar 4 leads to a G^7 and a cadence on C. D minor in the beginning key of F is VI. In C, it is II and moves effectively to V and then on to I in C.

ANDANTE

Pleyel

Learn this basic chord pattern which illustrates a modulation to the dominant key via II^6-I_4^6-V^7-I in the new key. The old key is established with tonic and dominant harmony. Transpose this pattern to F, G and other keys.

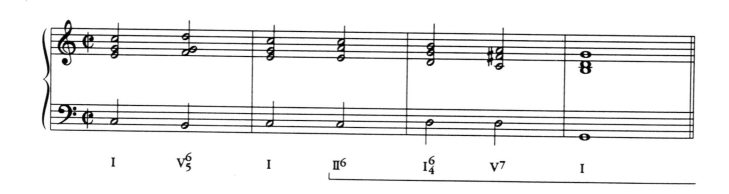

$$\text{I} \qquad V_5^6 \qquad \text{I} \qquad II^6 \qquad I_4^6 \qquad V^7 \qquad \text{I}$$

Modulation to the Relative Minor

The most direct route to take when modulating is to proceed to the dominant of the new tonality with no other harmonies preceding that dominant. Such is the case with *Solomon Levi* below. Also take note of the temporary shift to the dominant key in the bottom system, just prior to the return.

SOLOMON LEVI

Traditional

D.C. al fine

Learn the chord pattern below which moves from major to relative minor. Transpose this pattern to other keys.

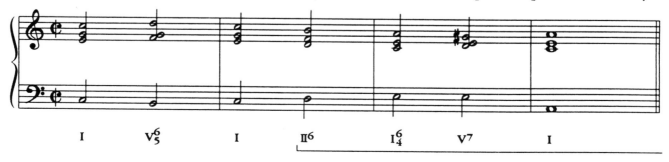

I   V$_5^6$ I   II^6 I$_4^6$ V^7 I

Modulation to the Relative Major

Major and minor scales which share the same key signatures are called relative scales. Study the excerpt below from Burgmüller's *Arabesque* to see how the tonality shifts from A minor to the key of C. The manner is direct. Burgmüller establishes the new key (C) by using I_4^6-V^7-I; the I in A minor becomes VI in C major.

ARABESQUE

Burgmüller

Learn the chord pattern below which moves from minor to the relative major. Transpose this pattern to selected keys.

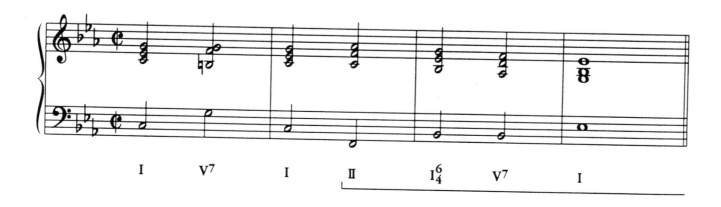

I   V⁷   I   II   I⁶₄   V⁷   I

Music for Reading and Analysis

In the *Russian Song*, determine the transition chords used in moving from C to A minor.

RUSSIAN SONG

Transpose to B♭

In the *British Melody*, notice the brief shift to the relative major key and then a return to G minor.

BRITISH MELODY

Transpose to Fm

Chording

Learn the chordal accompaniment to *Peg O' My Heart*. Analyze the sevenths used in the harmonization.

PEG O' MY HEART

words by **Alfred Bryan**
music by **Fred Fisher**

Ensemble

WHEN THE SAINTS
Secondo–Teacher or Student

arr. Caramia

WHEN THE SAINTS
Primo–Student or Teacher

arr. Caramia

MODULATING

Secondo–Teacher or Student

Céline Bussières-Lessard

D.S. al fine

MODULATING
Primo-Student or Teacher

Céline Bussières-Lessard

D.S. al fine

TANGO

Secondo

Ben Blozan

Allegro

TANGO

Primo

Ben Blozan

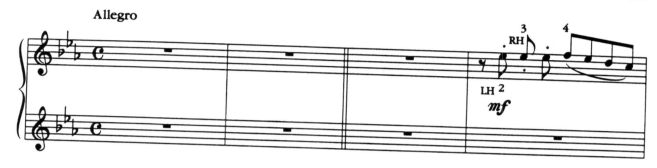

Secondo

dolce

con pedale

sfz

Repertoire

Find brief key shifts in the following selections.

SONATINA Op. 36 No. 1
First Movement

Clementi

CONTREDANCE

Mozart

MINUET

From Leopold Mozart's
"Notebook for Wolfgang"

D.C. al fine

SONATINA IN G
Second Movement

Beethoven

Allegretto

Theory Review

Build scale tone 7th chords in the following key. Label by Roman numeral (under the bass) and letter name (above the soprano) each chord and its quality.

Build 7th chords on the various tones given below. Double check the chord quality before notating each 7th chord.

Ebmaj7   Amin7   Gm7(b5)   Fdim7   D7

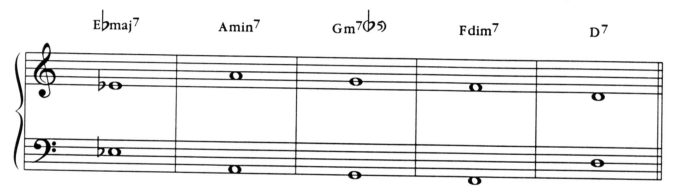

Analyze the following chords. Label them by letter name.

Ab7 ___ ___ ___ ___ ___ ___ ___

Complete the following sequence of seventh chords.

Fmaj7   Bbmaj7   Em7(b5)   Am7   Dm7   Gm7   C7   F

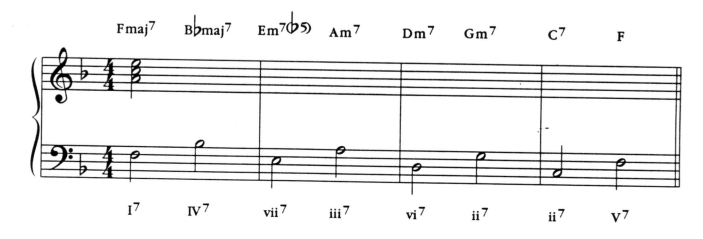

I7   IV7   vii7   iii7   vi7   ii7   ii7   V7

Improvising

The various patterns below have been extracted from chord patterns or pieces in this chapter. Use these backgrounds as a springboard to improvising melodies in the right hand. Repeat each pattern several times until a satisfactory conclusion is reached.

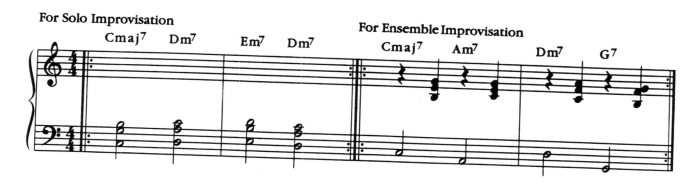

Improvise a twelve bar blues melody over the LH pattern from Caramia's *Slow Blues*. Notate your best effort.

Develop the following musical idea. Improvise several phrases in the RH over the bass pattern.

Technic

Study in Sevenths covers various forms of arpeggiated seventh chords. Play the exercise slowly and "feel" the position of each chord pattern. The fingering remains the same for each measure. Transpose to selected keys.

STUDY IN SEVENTHS

Alexander

SUGGESTED QUIZ TOPICS — CHAPTER EIGHT

1. Build seventh chords on the scale degrees of E♭, A♭, A and E. Identify each chord by letter name symbol and quality.

2. Build the following seventh chords in this order: Maj⁷, Dom⁷, Min⁷, Min⁷(♭5) and Dim⁷. Be able to do this on six different tones.

3. Demonstrate an understanding of jazz idioms by playing *Pattern in Color* or *Seventh Heaven* (Sevenths), one blues piece (*Slow Blues* or *Blue Waltz*) and the *Rag* (ragtime rhythms).

4. Play one or two of the harmonized early popular tunes from the following list: 1) *For Me and My Gal,* 2) *You Said Something,* 3) *Smiles,* 4) *Poor Butterfly* or 5) *(Back Home Again In) Indiana.*

5. Be able to modulate to the dominant and relative minor using the chord patterns found on pages 248 and 249.

6. Chord the accompaniment to *Peg O' My Heart,* pages 252-253.

7. Play one duet from the Ensemble section, pages 254-261.

8. Play one solo from the Repertoire section, pages 262-267.

A Glossary of Musical Terms and Signs

Accelerando (accel.) ..... gradually increasing the speed or tempo.

Adagio .... slow, but quicker than Largo and Lento.

Allegretto .... lively; slower than Allegro.

Allegro .... quick; lively; rapid.

Andante .... moderately slow, but flowing easily (walking tempo).

Andantino .... a little faster than Andante.

Animato (Animando) .. lively; animated.

Arpeggio .... playing the notes of a chord consecutively (harp style).

Assez vif (vite) .... rather quickly.

A tempo .... in time. A return to the original tempo after a ritard or accelerando.

Cadence .... a close in melody or harmony. The end of a phrase.

Cantabile .... in singing style.

Cesura (//) .... a complete separation.

Chorale .... old form of psalm or hymn tune of the early German Protestant Church.

Coda .... a passage added to the end of a composition.

Con .... with.

Con anima .... with animation; life.

Con brio .... with fire; spirit.

Con fuoco .... with fire.

Con moto .... with motion.

Con Spirito (spiritoso) with spirit.

Crescendo (cresc.) .... gradually becoming louder.

Da Capo (D.C.) .... from the beginning.

Dal Segno (D.S.) .... repeat from the sign.

Decrescendo (decresc.) gradually becoming softer.

Diminuendo (dim.) ..... gradually softer.

Dolce .... sweetly; softly.

Ecossaise .... a lively Scotch dance.

Espressivo .... expressive.

Fermata .... a pause or hold.

Fine .... the end.

Forte (f) .... loud.

Fortissimo (ff) .... very loud.

German Dance .... a dance related to the Minuet, in $\frac{3}{4}$ time.

Giocoso .... happy; playful; mirthful.

Grave .... slow; solemn.

Grazioso .... gracefully; elegantly.

Largo .... slow; stately.

Legato .... smooth; connected; bound together. The reverse of staccato.

Leggeramente .... lightly.

Leggiero .... light; rapid; delicate.

Lento (Lent, Fr.) .... slow, between Largo and Adagio.

Loco .... play as written.

Maestoso .... majestic; dignified.

Marcato .... marked; emphasized.

Marcia .... march.

Meno .... less.

Menuet (Minuet) .... a slow, stately dance in $\frac{3}{4}$ time.

Mezzo .... half.

Mezzo Forte (mf) .... half or moderately loud.

Mezzo Piano (mp) .... half or moderately soft.

Moderato .... moderate.

Molto .... very much; exceedingly.

Mosso .... motion; movement.

Ostinato .... recurring figure, usually in the bass.

Pastoral (Pastorale) .... portraying a rustic or rural scene.

Pensieroso .... thoughtfully; pensively.

Pesante .... heavy.

Piano (p) .... soft.

Pianissimo (pp) .... very soft.

piu .... more.

Poco .... a little, rather.

Poco a poco .... little by little; by degrees.

Portato .... disconnected; neither staccato nor legato.

Presto .... fast.

Rallentando (rall.) .... gradually becoming slower.

Religioso .... in a religious manner.

Ritardando (rit.) .... retarding; getting slower and slower.

Rubato .... robbed; stolen. The rhythmic flow is interrupted by dwelling slightly on some melodic notes and slightly hurrying others.

Sempre .... always; continually.

Sforzando (sfz or sf) .. forced; a strong accent.

Simile .... the same.

Sostenuto .... sustained; unhurried.

Staccato .... detached; separated.

Subito .... suddenly.

Tranquillo .... tranquil; calm.

Troppo .... too much.

Vivace .... animated; lively.

Vivo .... lively; briskly.

272

SIGNS

sharp .... ♯	accent and sustain ....
flat .... ♭	a break or breath mark .... ,
natural .... ♮	rolled chord ....
double sharp .... ×	tenuto mark – sustain ....
double flat .... ♭♭	triplet ....
fermata .... 𝄐	accent .... >
repeat sign .... ‖: :‖	endings .... 1. 2.
tie	pedal .... Ped. ✤
slur	acciaccatura ....
staccato	8va
portato (See Glossary)	swing (♪♪) ....

APPENDIX

B Scales and Arpeggios

Major Scales – Two Octaves

C Major

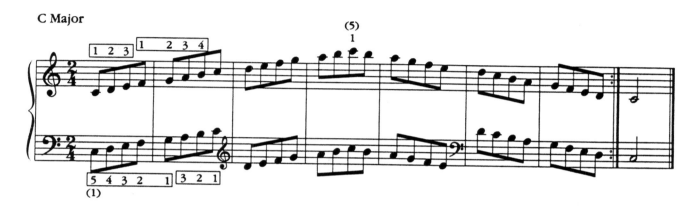

When putting hands together, notice that thumbs fall on the tonic, and the third fingers play together on the third and sixth scale degrees. This will hold true for the scales of C, G, D, A and E.

G Major

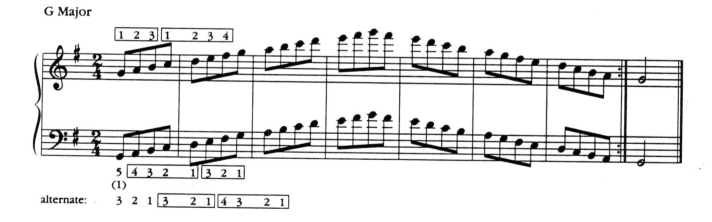

D Major

274

A Major

alternate:

E Major

B Major

F Sharp Major

C Sharp Major

Flat Scale Fingerings

Study the following principles which apply to fingering flat scales. (1) The fourth finger of the right hand will always play B flat. Knowing this makes it possible to figure out any right hand flat scale fingering. In any flat key, simply place the right hand fourth finger on B flat and let the other fingers fall on adjacent scale tones in the key. Determine the groups of three and four. (2) The fingering pattern in the left hand for the keys of B flat, E flat, A flat and D flat is 3 2 1 4 3 2 1. This fingering may also be used for the F scale, but the traditional fingering for the left hand is like C major (5) 4 3 2 1 3 2 1. The fourth finger of the left hand always adds a new flat for each new key, when using the 3 2 1 4 3 2 1 pattern. The order of the scales below begins with F and proceeds through the circle of fourths, e.g., F, B flat, E flat and so on. Learn these scales gradually and be guided by your teacher as to various ways to practice the scales.

F Major

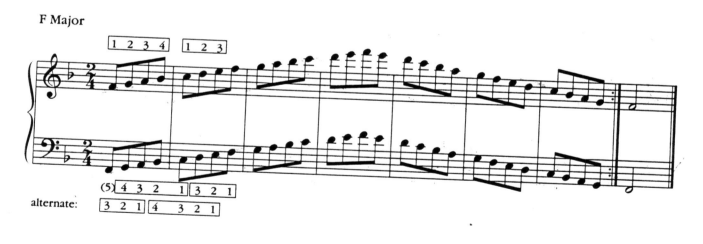

alternate: 3 2 1 4 3 2 1

B Flat Major

E Flat Major

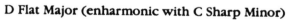

A Flat Major

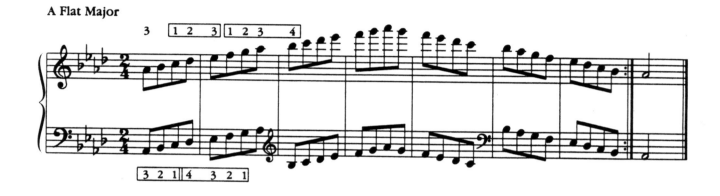

D Flat Major (enharmonic with C Sharp Minor)

G Flat Major (enharmonic with F Sharp Major)

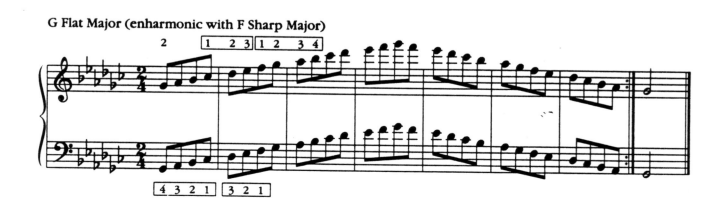

C Flat Major (enharmonic with B Major)

Major Arpeggios – Two Octaves

Add arpeggio practice immediately following scale practice. Learn the fingerings carefully. Pass the thumb under quickly.

C Major   G Major

D Major   A Major

E Major   B Major

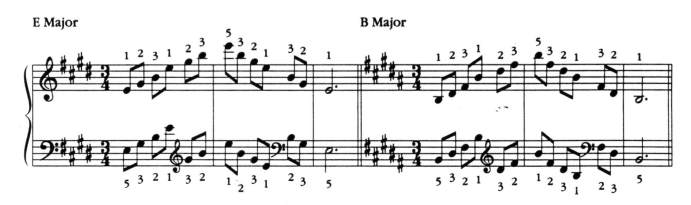

F Sharp Major
(G Flat Major)

D Flat Major
(C Sharp Major)

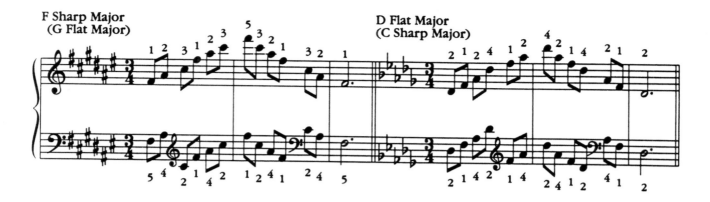

A Flat Major

E Flat Major

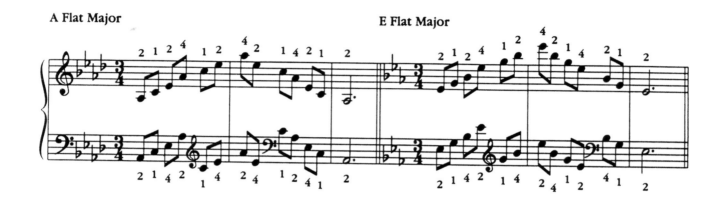

B Flat Major

F Major

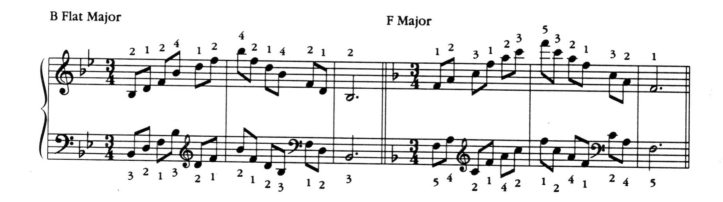

C Two Patriotic Songs

Write in a suitable fingering for each hand. Compare this harmony to a chord progression studied earlier: I–vi–IV–ii^6–I$^6_4$–V^7–I. Write the chord symbols beneath the bass line. *America* has many examples of *passing tones*—non-harmonic tones passing between chord tones.

AMERICA

Moderato

Carey

My coun - try 'tis of thee, Sweet land of lib - er - ty,

mf

Of thee I sing. Land where my fa - thers died! Land of the

Pil - grim's pride! From ev - 'ry moun - tain side, Let free - dom ring!

THE STAR-SPANGLED BANNER

Smith

D Holiday Music

I SAW THREE SHIPS

England
arr. Heitler and Lyke

With spirit

I saw three ships come sail- ing in On Christ- mas Day, on Chrit- mas Day, I

saw three ships come sail- ing in On Christ- mas Day in the morn - ing.

PAT-A-PAN

French Carol
arr. by Heitler and Lyke

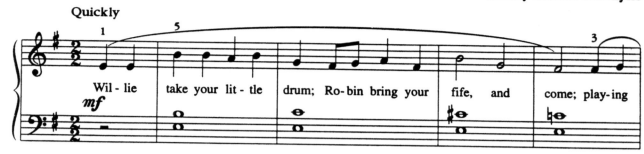

Wil - lie take your lit - tle drum; Ro - bin bring your fife, and come; play-ing

on the fife and drum, Tu - re - lu - re - lu, pat - a - pat - a - pan, We'll make

mus - ic loud and gay, For our Christ - mas hol - i - day.

O COME LITTLE CHILDREN

German Carol
arr. by Heitler and Lyke

O come lit - tle child - ren, O come one and all, O

come to the man - ger in Beth - le - hem's stall, And

see with re - joic - ing the glo - ri - ous sight, The

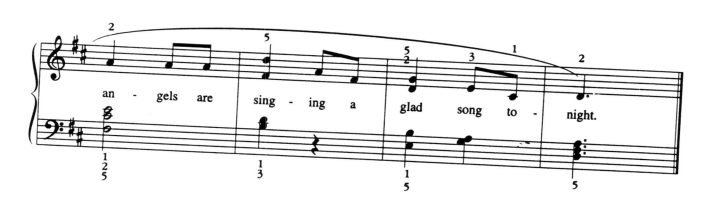

an - gels are sing - ing a glad song to - night.

UP ON THE HOUSETOP

Words and Music by
Benjamin R. Hanby
arr. by Heitler and Lyke

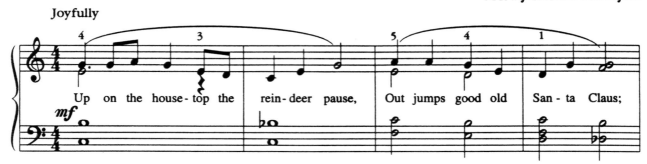

Up on the house-top the rein-deer pause, Out jumps good old San-ta Claus;

Down through the chim-ney with lots of toys, All for the lit-tle ones Christ-mas joys.

Ho, ho, ho, Who would-n't go! Ho, ho, ho, Who would-n't go!

Up on the house-top, click, click, click, Down through the chim-ney with good Saint Nick.

SILENT NIGHT

words by **Joseph Mohr**
music by **Franz Gruber**
arr. by Heitler and Lyke

JINGLE BELLS

words and music by
James Pierpont
arr. by Heitler and Lyke

Dash-ing through the snow, in a one horse o-pen sleigh, o'er the fields we go, Laugh-ing all the way;

Bells on bob-tail ring, Mak-ing spir-its bright, Oh, what fun it is to sing a sleigh-ing song to-night.

Jin-gle bells, Jin-gle bells, Jin-gle all the way,— Oh, what fun it is to ride in a one-horse o-pen sleigh!—

Jin-gle bells, Jin-gle bells, Jin-gle all the way,— Oh, what fun it is to ride in a one horse o-pen sleigh!

WHAT CHILD IS THIS

English Carol
arr. by Heitler and Lyke

THE FIRST NOËL

arr. Lyke

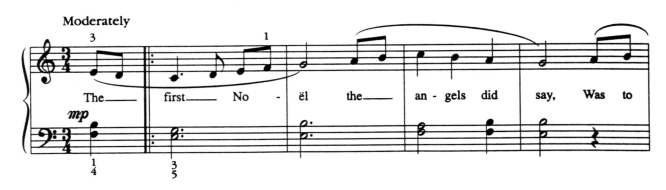

The___ first___ No - ël the___ an - gels did say, Was to

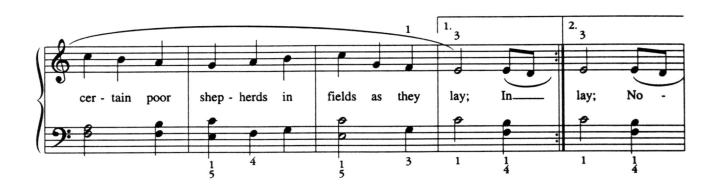

cer - tain poor shep - herds in fields as they lay; In___ lay; No -

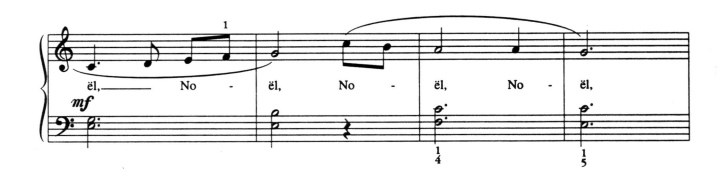

ël,_____ No - ël, No - ël, No - ël,

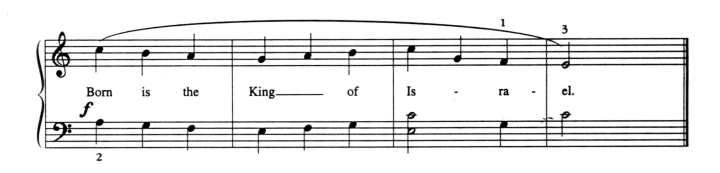

Born is the King___ of Is - ra - el.

GOOD KING WENCESLAS

arr. Lyke

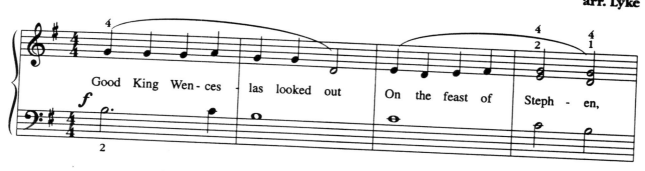

Good King Wen - ces - las looked out On the feast of Steph - en,

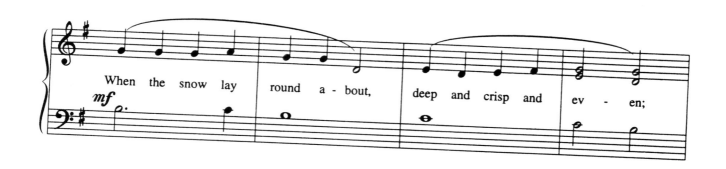

When the snow lay round a - bout, deep and crisp and ev - en;

Bright - ly shone the moon that night, Tho' the frost was cru - el,

When a poor man came in sight, Gath - 'ring win - ter fu - el.

TOYLAND

words *by* **Glen MacDonald**
music by **Victor Herbert**
arr. Lyke

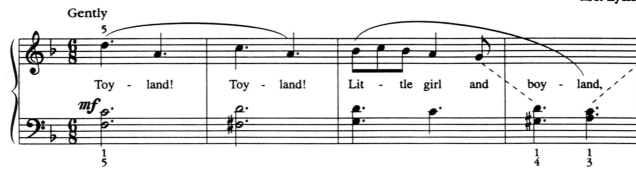

Toy - land! Toy - land! Lit - tle girl and boy - land,

While you dwell with - in it___ you are ev - er hap - py then.

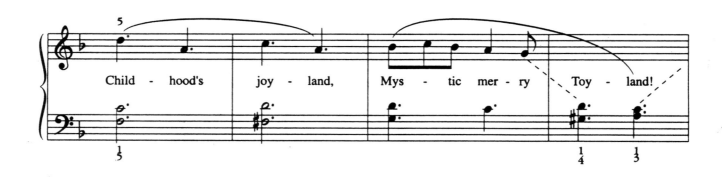

Child - hood's joy - land, Mys - tic mer - ry Toy - land!

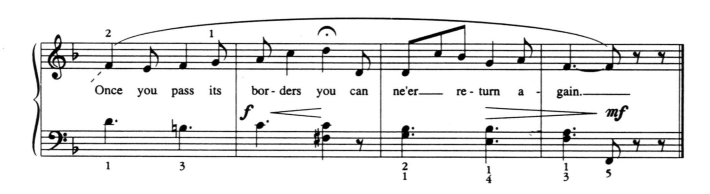

Once you pass its bor - ders you can ne'er___ re - turn a - gain.___

APPENDIX E Piano Literature

294